MANTRI PRAGADA MAR

MW01673965

INVESTMENT, TRADE AND BUSINESS

(Rates vary, as per prevailing land and flat costs)

REAL ESTATE TRENDS AND BOOM

(Rates vary, as per prevailing land and flat costs)

PROPERTY TRENDS @ HYDERABAD - INDIA

HYDERABAD (TELANGANA STATE) INDIA
MOBILE: +91 9951038802
Email: mrkndyl@gmail.com

REAL ESTATE TRENDS & BOOM
PROPERTY TRENDS @ HYDERABAD - INDIA

MANTRI PRAGADA MARKANDEYULU
[B. Com, DipBM, PG.DipCA, DipCP.]

HYDERABAD (TELANGANA STATE) INDIA

MOBILE: (+91) 9951038802
Email: mrkndyl@gmail.com

REAL ESTATE TRENDS AND BOOM
(Rates vary, as per prevailing land and flat costs)

INDEX

25) **DESTINATION BACHUPALLY**
26) **DESTINATION MADHAPUR**
27) **DESTINATION GACHIBOWLI**
28) **DESTINATION MIYAPUR**
29) **DESTINATION BALANAGAR**
30) **DESTINATION NALLAGNDLA**
31) **DESTINATION NARSINGI**
32) **DESTINATION KONDAPUR**
33) **DESTINATION L B NAGAR**
34) **DESTINATION KOMPALLY**
35) **DESTINATION CHANDA NAGAR**
36) **DESTINATION EAST MAREDPALLY**
37) **DESTINATION LINGAMPALLY**
38) **DESTINATION NALLAGANDLA**
39) **DESTUBATUIB NAGOLE**
40) **DESTINATION VANASTHALIPURAM**
41) **DESTINATION ADIBATLA**
42) **DESTINATION HAYAT NAGAR**
43) **DESTINATION RAJENDRA NAGAR**

HOT PLACES AT HYDERABAD – INDIA

01) **DESTINATION KUKATPALLY**
02) **DESTINATION MANIKONDA**
03) **DESTINATION UPPAL**
04) **DESTINATION PUPPALAGUDA – NARSINGI**
05) **DESTINATION KHAJA GUDA**
06) **DESTINATION FINANCIAL DISTRICT**
07) **DESTINATION BACHUPALLY**
08) **DESTINATION MADHAPUR**
09) **DESTINATION GACHIBOWLI**
10) **DESTINATION MIYAPUR**
11) **DESTINATION BALANAGAR**
12) **DESTINATION NALLAGNDLA**
13) **DESTINATION NARSINGI**

14) **DESTINATION KONDAPUR**
15) **DESTINATION L B NAGAR**
16) **DESTINATION KOMPALLY**
17) **DESTINATION CHANDA NAGAR**
18) **DESTINATION EAST MAREDPALLY**
19) **DESTINATION LINGAMPALLY**
20) **DESTINATION NALLAGANDLA**
21) **DESTUBATUIB NAGOLE**
22) **DESTINATION VANASTHALIPURAM**
23) **DESTINATION ADIBATLA**
24) **DESTINATION HAYAT NAGAR**
25) **DESTINATION RAJENDRA NAGAR**

HYDERABAD [TELANGANA STATE – INDIA]

(Rates vary, as per prevailing land and flat costs)

QUICK TAKE

HYDERABAD (TELANGANA STATE) – INDIA
City's master plan to be ready next year

Main Feature is To Bring Existing Plans on to a Single Hassle-Free Platform

If everything goes well, Hyderabad Metropolitan Region (HMR) will have its integrated master plan in place in early 2017 year. The Hyderabad Metropolitan Development Authority (HMDA) took up integration of five past masers plans a few months ago to bring uniformity in land use patterns and zoning regulations and incorporating various projects.

The draft master plan will be published after getting a clearance from the municipal administration and urban development department soon. Following this, objections and suggestions from general public will be sought for a month.

Officials said integration of the past master plans was necessitated as different regions have different zoning regulations and land uses. The discrepancies emerged as a major concern for HMDA while granting permissions for new buildings and layouts which were not reflected in existing master plans. The five master plans, prepared in the past decade, were meant for different periods.

The new integrated master plan is being readied for the next 25 years i.e. till 2041. As per estimates, population in Hyderabad Metropolitan Region will reach 2 crore from existing 1.02 crore in this period.

The main feature of the integrated master plan is bringing existing plans onto a single platform along with GIS data that will help make approvals hassle-free. Citizens in the near future can get land use details of a particular survey number and also check whether they can get permission for a house from just the click of a mouse.

MASTER PLAN

The HMDA this June 2016 began integration of five past master plans – 20-year old Hyderabad Urban Development Authority plan that expires in 2021 year, the Cyberabad Development Authority (CDA) and Hyderabad Airport Development Authority (HADA) expiring in the year 2021, Municipal Corporation (MCH) and extended Hyderabad Metropolitan Development Authority (Metropolitan Development Authority) set to expire in the year 2031.

- **New Master Plan will expire in the year 2041**
- **Total HMDA area: 7,257 sq.km**
- **Cyberabad Development Authority (CDA) area 51 sq.km**
- **Hyderabad Airport Development Authority (HADA) area: 171 sq km**
- **Metropolitan Development Plan for extended HUDA area: 5985 sq km**
- **M/s LEA Associates South Asia Pvt Ltd is preparing the new master plan.**
- **Over 4,000 suggestions received from architects, urban planners, real estate developers and officials were considered for the new plan.**

As of now, there are 24 types of land uses including residential, commercial, industrial, manufacturing, conservation and mixed use. These categories will be clubbed into 12 uses. Some land uses such as industrial and manufacturing are not necessary. There will be only industrial use now, certain land uses in Cyberabad Development Authority (CDA) like Central Business District are irrelevant now.

In the integrated master plan, HMDA was asked by the government to incorporate and earmark some areas for major projects such Information Technology Investment Region (ITIR) and Hyderabad-Warangal Industrial Corridor. Interestingly, the HMDA earmarked some locations as 'No Development Area' where no development is permitted. The areas would be used for disaster management when necessary.

HYDERABAD CITY REALITY
WATER CONNECTIVITY WELCOMED.

HMWSSB'S move to provide water to areas beyond GHMC and around ORR welcomed by builders and residents.

The recent announcement of Hyderabad Metropolitan Water Supply and Sewerage Board (HMWSSB) supplying water beyond GHMC limits to areas in and around Outer Ring Road (ORR) has brought a smile on the faces of city realtors.

A part of the ambitious Telangana Water Grid project, the arrangement will provide drinking water to 12 mandals. Areas such as Saroornagar, Maheshwaram, Rajendranagar, Shamshabad, Hayatnagar, Ibrahimpatnam, Ghatkesar, Keesara, Shameerpet, Medchal, Quthbullapur, Patancheru and Ramachandrapuram will come under the purview of the arrangement.

With most of the mentioned areas being the new real estate hotspots, the project will give a huge boost to the real estate scene of the city.

This announcement has been a great step towards CM's promise to bring drinking water to every household. From the market point of view, this will be very convenient for end users and make their lives comfortable.

Shortage of drinking water in different areas has been a perennial issue in several parts of the city which has been a hindrance for realtors with projects in such areas. The arrangement will help removing this obstacle, which can lead to a substantial increase in terms of sales. Telangana chapter says, Ground water level in certain areas is absolutely dismal. If the said plan is implemented properly, it not only helps the current residences in the area but also help in the sale of the existing projects there and give boost to developing projects in the areas. The rentals will also go high.

Regular availability of water is very essential for any real estate development. With depleting ground waters in Hyderabad, the announcement of HMWS to provide drinking water beyond GHMC limits is welcome news. With this initiative new projects can be taken up beyond GHMC limits. This helps in providing sustainable housing to a greater number of end users. This move also helps in decongesting the already clogged GHMC limits.

REAL ESTATE
PROPERTY TRENDS @ HYDERABAD - INDIA

(Rates vary, as per prevailing land and flat costs)

INVESTMENT, TRADE AND BUSINESS

The subject **REAL ESTATE** – PROPERTY & TRENDS (Investment, Trade, and Business & Trends) is very interesting one and the on-going buying and selling the properties often on profitable side for those who are in Real Estate business. The Real Estate Note gives elaborative details in the development areas at the Greater Hyderabad city of new Telangana State of India.

This is the time to acquire land & properties as the new Telangana State is fully encouraging the Investors for Trade, Business and Investment.

It is doubly sure to gain profits for those Investors who invest money especially in Real Estate business in very shorter period, as the State of Telangana is poised for quick and vast development in all the fields including infrastructure side.

It is hoped that buyers will soon realize this fast-developing Real Estate Trends and invest in this flourishing business.

MANTRI PRAGADA MARKANDEYULU
Author and Writer

MORE TAX BENEFITS FOR HOMEBUYERS EXPECTED

The Union Budget can hold some good news for homebuyers in the light of the changes expected with the demonetization.

The recent demonetization is expected to have a significant impact on the tax structures, going forward.

TOWARDS CASHLESS ECONOMY

There is a tremendous push to roué transactions through the banking system rather than on cash. With this, he GDP of the country is expected to increase in the long run.

Despite some challenges being experienced currently, the boost for the banking system, and the influx of cash into the economy, will push growth of the GDP.

WIDER TAX BASE

The demonetization is expected to widen the tax base, and prepare the ground for lower taxation, a lower inflation rate and a drop I the interest rates. More tax sops such as an increase in the deduction limit under Section 80C and an increase in the exemption limit against interest paid on a housing loan are expected. Some relaxation in the income tax slabs and the tax rates are also expected.

TAX RELIEF EXPECTED

It is important to note that this time the Union Budget announcement will come just before five States with population of around 250 million go to polls in 2017. The government is expected to provide some tax benefits in this Budget to ease the pain borne in general by the people as a fallout of the demonetization exercise. As the tax base expands, and more people come into the tax net, the government will ease out the tax complexities to encourage more compliance and user in a tax-friendly environment. This can happen with lower rates of income tax, covering a wider base.

Bringing down direct taxes will help in preventing growth in the parallel economy. When taxes are high, people try to avoid them. If taxes are reasonable and modest, there is lesser incentive to evade them. Further, a simple tax system will ensure more people follow in compliance.

===============

TAX SOPS, LOWER INTEREST RATES ON BUYERS' WISH LIST

With the Union Budget to be presented, expectations are high. Here are a few major ones of prospective homebuyers looking for initiatives in the Budget that will make that dream home more affordable.

The Union Budget for the financial year is scheduled to be presented in Parliament. As the Budget Day approaches every year, the expectations of prospective home buyers get stronger. There is plenty on the wish lists of individuals. The demonetization move in November 2016 is expected to have significant impact on the tax structures, going forward. In particular, homebuyers, who have already bought a property or are planning to buy one, have more hope with respect to deductions against **Income from House Property.**

Under the Income Tax Act, income from House Property is an important avenue for tax planning. Under the Act, any income earned from a house is subject to tax, provided certain conditions are met.

DEDUCTION AGAINST INTEREST PAID

Interest paid on a home loan constitutes a substantial part of an EMI, especially in the initial years of the loan tenure. Presently, the Income Tax Act allows a deduction against interest paid on a housing loan. The deduction was increased to Rs. 2 lakhs some time ago. In case of a self-occupied property, the deduction against interest is restricted to Rs. 2 lakhs. However, in case of a property that has been rented out, there is no limit on the deduction against interest.

One major expectation of homebuyers is the enhancement of this limit against interest paid on a home loan. An enhancement of this limit will go a long way in easing the tax burden of homebuyers.

DEDUCTION AGAINST PRINCIPAL REPAID

The Income Tax Act also allows a deduction of up to Rs. 1.50 lakhs under Section 80C towards repayment of principal amount of a home loan. A point to be noted is that the Section 80C deduction covers many amounts paid including contribution to Provident Fund, Public Provident Fund, investments in certain equity linked saving schemes, tax saving mutual funds, premium on insurance policies etc. This Section also covers payments made towards the construction or purchase of a residential property.

However, in most cases, hardly any eligible amount will be left over to claim as a deduction against the amount paid towards repayment of a loan's principal component. Clubbing this deduction under Section 80C is not much use as other saving instruments tend to exhaust the limit, in most cases.

So, there is a valid case for enhancement of the deduction limit under Section 80C towards the repayment of the principal component of a home loan. Considering the fact that this is an important part of acquisition of a property, even a separate Section for this deduction may be allowed.

REDUCTION IN STAMP DUTY

A long-pending demand has been a reduction in stamp duty on property transactions. Although this is a state subject, the central government can take measures to reduce it. By reducing the stamp duty rates on registration and transfer of property, the incentive to under-value the property by buyers will not be there. This will pave the way for more compliance and an increase in revenue for the government.

REDUCTION IN INTEREST RATES, MORE TAX SOPS

Another major expectation is lower interest rates. Homebuyers expect the government to initiate more steps towards a further reduction in the lending interest rates.

Also, homebuyers hope that the tax sops of this financial year are continued in the coming financial year as well Section 80EE, a new section that was introduced in the Union Budget 2016, enabled an additional deduction of up to

Rs. 50,000 against interest on a home loan sanctioned between April 1, 2016 and March 31, 2017, provided the value of the property purchased is less than Rs. 50 lakhs and the loan taken is less than Rs. 35 lakhs. It is expected that this benefit is continued and the coverage widened by enhancing the limit.

CAPITAL GAINS

Homebuyers also hope for some additional relief on capital gains earned on sale of a property, apart from the current avenues. The existing benefits were introduced a long time ago. There is a need now to extend the scope of the specified instruments and relax the stringent conditions to help claim more I exemptions and relief from capital gains tax.

FINANCIAL PLANNING IN ADVANCE IS IDEAL

THE BANK WILL DISBURSE THIS AMOUNT ONLY WHEN THE PROPERTY IS FINALISED AND IT HAS COMPLETED ITS LEGAL DUE DILIGENCE ON THE PROPERTY.

Finance is a critical aspect of a home purchase. This is the right time to begin on your financial planning if you are in the midst of closing in on a new home this festive season.

Many are planning to buy a house. This is an auspicious time when prospective homebuyers tie their purchases. The property prices re at attractive levels. On top of that, there are innumerable offers both from developers as well as from banks. Also, the Reserve Bank of India (RBI) has reduced the repo rate and indicated further cuts in the future. This will lead to lower interest rates for borrowers.

OFFERS GALORE

To cater to the demand and woo buyers, property developers have come out with new plans and incentives. Offers such as special launch prices, no EMIs till possession, free furnishing, modular kitchen complimentary, attractive gifts and so on are announced during the festive period. Also, backing the developers during the festive season rush, banks and home finance companies come out with new and innovative loan products to attract more borrowers. They tie up with developers and provide instant loan approvals. Further, schemes such as waiver of processing fee, special interest rate etc are launched.

TIME TO PLAN YOUR FINANCES

A prospective homebuyer has to plan the process of acquiring a home from short listing a property, generating the finances, legal scrutiny, availing a bank loan and so on. There is detailed paper work and need for planning at each stage. Apart from the legal matters, finance is a crucial factor for those planning to buy a home. Most homebuyers go in for a home loan from a bank. The interest rates are low and are expected to come down further in the near future. Also, there are tax incentives in case you opt for a home loan.

So, it makes sense to purchase a property with a home loan. You need to keep in mind that banks do not fund 100 percent of the purchase price. A bank usually funds 70-80 percent of the value, based on the applicant's financial position. A bank considers your incomes, liabilities, existing loans, credit history etc to decide on the loan amount you are eligible for. The rest of the cost has to be met out of your own resources. So, you need to plan your finances for the purchase judiciously.

PLAN FOR LOAN

In case you are on the lookout for a home or have already shortlisted a property for purchase, it makes sense to apply for an in-principal approval of a bank loan. A bank needs time to evaluate your creditworthiness. You can approach different banks and check your loan eligibility, interest rate offered, terms etc. Once you identify the most suitable bank, you can ask for an in-principal approval. Here, the bank completes its credit evaluation and other formalities as well as due diligence related to you verifying your ID, employment etc. Based on your income and other factors, it will issue you in-principal approval, specifying the amount up to which it can provide you a loan. This gives you an assurance of the amount of bank finance you will get. The bank will disburse this amount only when the property is finalized and it has completed its legal due diligence on the property. This approval is usually valid for 90 to 180 days.

PLAN FOR DOWN PAYMENT

You need to plan for some funds that you will have to raise on your own. This is the component of the cost of the house that the bank will not provide for.

You can park the funds in a fixed deposit that you can encash and transfer into your bank account immediately. In case you are borrowing from your Provident Fund account or against an insurance policy, it will take some time. In this case, you need to put in the application well in advance as the process may take 7-10 days.

Yu also need to plan I advance I case you plan to sell shares or mutual fund units as it depend on the market conditions. It is to be kept in mind that the funds so accumulated should be deposited in a safe avenue. A bank account or bank fixed deposit is ideal as these are highly liquid and safe. The bank from which you are availing a home loan will release its share of the finance only once you have arranged for your share too.

Overall, the points to be kept in mind are you need to plan and arrange for funds well in advance. Equally important is planning the repayment of the home loan over its tenure. You should be able to pay the EMIs as well as meet the household expenses over the tenure of the home loan comfortably and without undue pressure, give its long term

===============

TIME TO START PLANNING YOUR HOME PURCHASE

The Union Budget is expected to bring good news for prospective homebuyers. Getting started early on the planning will help you get a good deal.

Budget 2017 is around the corner. This time, there are strong expectations of more benefits for homebuyers with higher tax breaks. Also, there are expectations of some relief in income tax and this in turn will leave prospective homebuyers with more cash in hand. This is welcome news. With property prices hovering at attractive levels, prospective buyers will find this an opportune moment to buy a home. In the wake of demonetization, and the cash crunch with the new notes taking some time to reach the banks and ATMs, this will come as a trigger.

The home loan interest rates began on a downward trend recently and it is likely to continue. The sentiment is to continue. The sentiment is bound to look up as prospective homebuyers find their affordability factor going up with cheaper home loans, more tax sops and attractive property prices, all adding up to make this one of the best market conditions in recent times.

While the numbers will be out only on February lst, and the exact amount you will get in additional tax benefits can be computed only then, it is time to get some spade work done if you have been planning to buy a home. A significant number of fence-sitters jumping into the fray post the Union Budget will push the market sentiment up a bit. So, some homework now will help you make a more informed choice two weeks later. Here are some pointers:

ARRIVE AT YOUR BUDGET

While the Budget will be presented in Parliament on February 1, it will come into effect from April 1. This means you have a good two months to evaluate the implications of the Budget on your home loan after it is announced.

You can begin on the planning right now. Generate an income and expense statement with projected income through the new financial year. Further fine tuning can be easily made after February 1.

Ensure you include all estimated incomes such as salary, returns from investments etc. Deduct from these projected expenses. Include expenses such as insurance premium, one-time expenses such as a car purchase that may arise, monthly savings including savings in a contingency fund etc. You will get a rough idea of the sort of budget you have for your new home.

Draw up a statement in detail listing all these incomes and expenses. Here, factor I the EMI including the tax benefits as they stand now. This can be updated after the Budget is announced. Given the strong sentiment in the market expecting higher tax breaks in the coming financial year, your statement in all probability will look better after February 1.

Once the final picture is clear with the Budget, begin shopping for a home loan. Track the market carefully as many financial institutions are bringing down their interest rates. Go through the terms and conditions closely and pick one that is most attractive If you choose your financial institution and loan scheme well, the overall cost of finance will be the minimum. It therefore makes immense sense to send time and shop for your home loan. Beginning now on the planning will afford you the luxury of more time to spend on evaluating the various options available.

EVALUATE PROPERTIES

If you haven't been evaluating properties, the sooner you begin the better. This becomes easier if done once you have arrived at your budget for the new home. With your budget clear, you can shortlist a few locations and projects. You can then begin visiting each of the projects on your list to finalize the one you feel is idea.

======

TOP RESIDENTIAL AREAS TODAY

Buying a house needs a lot of planning and thought. Here a few things that one need to consider before taking the step.

Hyderabad market is looking up and barring one locality, Chandanagar, all the localities have witnessed price increment ranging from 1.6 per cent to 5 per cent. Interestingly, the trend of property price increment is not restricted to just these end areas in Hyderabad. The City Index for Hyderabad reflects price movement across 26 prominent localities. "The Jul-Sep 2016 quarter had more localities with price increment than decline. At least 69% localities saw an average price increase of 3.4%, pushing up the Apr-Jun 2016 Index by slightly more than 3%. The balance 31% localities saw price drop of 3.6%, pushing down the Apr-Jun 2016 Index marginally leading to the City Index witnessing 3% increase in the Jul-Sep 2016 quarter."

The list of preferred localities of Hyderabad begins with the ones with per square feet area cost ranging between INR 3000-4000. Sainikpuri tops the list of 10 localities due to its affordable property values and the range of properties that it offers for various home buyers.

The locality has registered price increment of 3.7 per cent in this quarter. One can buy 1 BHK flats sized 525-895 sq ft in the range of INR 6-14 lakh. However, for a 2 BHK flat sized 650-1450 sq ft, one would have to pay INR 17-39 lakh. If aspiring a spacious 3 BHK flat then one can get in the size range of 850-2250 sq ft in h budget range of INR 27-63 lakh.

Sainikpuri's connectivity has also led to its popularity. One can easily reach this area from Hyderabad and Secunderabad through roads and railways. While the Secunderabad Railway Station is around 35 minutes' drive (13 km) via Krishna Deva Raya Road and Moula Ali flyover. The IT hub at Pocharum is also 30-35 minutes' drive away from here.

Second on the list is Kukatpally, which is located near Hitec City and is no longer an affordable destination in Hyderabad. Kukatpally has moved over its image of offering houses only in the budget segment. Today, its market offers various property types at different ranges and that attracts the interest of home buyers.

Kukatpally witnessed a price increment of 3.2 per cent in the last quarter. A 1 BHK flat in 450-720 sq ft size can be bought in INR 9.60 lakh – INR 22.40 lakh, while a 2 BHK unit sized 684 to 1640 sq ft can be bought for INR 22.50-52.50 lakh. A 3 BHK flat sized 905 to 2237 sq ft is in the market for INR 37-86.80 lakh.

Kukatpally has an extensive road network and therefore offers good connectivity with all the major localities.

The Mumbai Highway passes through the center of the locality and gives good connectivity with places, such as Ameerpet, Banjara Hills, Moosapet and Miyapur.

The third locality is Miyapur, which has seen a dynamic rise in the real estate market. Part of Greater Hyderabad Municipal Corporation, Miyapur is a preferred choice for home buyers as it is strategically located at a distance of about 10 km from Hitech city. Being an affordable residential place near an IT sector, Miyapur is the preferred destination for IT professionals in Hyderabad. Miyapur has seen a price increment of 1.6 per cent this quarter. One can buy l BHK flat in 413-880 sq ft in INR 9 lakh-21 lakh.

2 BHK flats are mostly in the size of 680-1555 sq ft and in the price range of INR 17.40-40.60 lakh. For a spacious 3 BHK flat in sizes such as 1077-2215 sq ft, one would have to shell out INR 30.48 lakh to INR 71.12 lakh.

======

SOME POINTERS FOR HOME-BUYERS

Here are some developments prospective homebuyers need to track closely.

Last year was an eventful one for the realty sector. And 2007 promises to be no different. All the measures initiated towards boosting the sector in 2016 will yield results in 2017 and onwards. So, prospective homebuyers need to track developments closely.

RERA SET FOR IMPLEMENTATION

Firstly, The Real Estate Regulation Act (RERA) will be implemented by the States during this year. The Act specifies numerous provisions protecting the interests of property buyers. It will bring about more transparency in dealings. There are many legal remedies provided by the Act for buyers.

GST ON THE ANVIL

The GST (Goods and Services Tax) system is set to be implemented this year. This is by far rated as one of the most significant changes in the tax structure ever brought about. The GST Act is all set to come to center stage in 2017.
Once implemented, it will bring about sweeping changes in the tax arena. GST is expected to benefit the real estate industry significantly. It will solve many of the challenges faced by the real estate sector and help in boosting the sector onto a growth path.

The real estate industry contributes around eight percent to India's GDP. The sector is expected to benefit in the long term on account of rationalization in tax related compliances and slated gains in related sectors such as cement, steel, IT and BFSI (Banking, financial services and insurance). Under the GST system, developers will have a lower burden of tax on inputs such as cement and steel, as tax credits will be available for a set off at various stages.

HIGHER TAX BENEFITS EXPECTED.

There are strong expectations of the government enhancing the limit for tax deduction against interest paid on a housing loan Further, there is a demand for a separate section for deduction against the principal rapid on a home loan, rather than clubbing it along with other deductions under Section 80C.

HOUSING FOR ALL

The government has reiterated its support to the "Housing for All by 2022" project. This is likely gone get a further boost in terms of additional tax sops for budget housing to be made available to homebuyers of such properties. In addition, builders are also likely to get tax incentives for developing budget housing complexes.

In the last Union Budget, the government announced 100 percent deduction against profits on an undertaking of such a housing project. The Housing for All initiate is expected to be given impetus by extending more tax benefits to homebuyers this year.

Last year's Budget announced an additional Rs. 50,000 tax deduction on interest paid on a loan of less than Rs. 35 lakhs and for a house valued below Rs. 50 lakhs. The deduction may now be increased and could include all home loans for first-time buyers. This will encourage more to purchase houses.

TO KEEP HOUSE PRICES IN CHECK, CONSTRUCT MORE ROADS

The co-relation between building road infrastructure and restricting house prices to moderate levels in Indian metros.

It is not wealth that built our roads but roads that built our wealth. This line by former American President John F Kennedy holds true not only for the US but also India. Road infrastructure seems to be closely linked to residential price movements. Length of road construction is known to have a direct bearing on real estate. More importantly, it is equally vital in potentially lowering average house prices, particularly in urban areas.

As regards lengths increase, connectivity improves across a wider geography – thereby attracting new project launches at lower price points. This can reduce prices in urban agglomerations. If more roads are constructed in rural areas, price rise in urban cities could be restricted to moderate levels. This would help increase affordable housing project near the metros.

Currently, the only solution to the problem of urban housing shortage in Indian cities is building new infrastructure to connect more precincts to the city center. This theory becomes clearer when we compare the pan-India average residential price growth to the total length of road constructed in India annually which is released by the Ministry of Roads.

Not surprisingly, there was a strong inverse correlation between the two indicators. It suggests that when new roads are constructed across rural and urban areas, the spread of development happens over a wider geography. This can potentially bring down the premium that certain urban agglomerations command for having better connectivity. This could be par5tifularly true for infrastr5ucture-starved cities in India such as Mumbai and Bengaluru.

Fortunately, road infrastructure has emerged as a key focus area for the current government. According to media reports earlier this year, the road transport and highways ministry has set an ambitious target of laying more than 40 km of roads every day in 2016-17 – more than double the current pace. The construction target too has been set at 15,000 km against the 6,000 km constructed last year.

The Indian government plans to invest INR 3 trillion (US$ 44.73 billion) for developing 35,000 km of roads across the country, of which 21,000 km will be economic corridors and 14,000 km will be feeder routes. This is expected to improve freight movement, ease traffic bottlenecks and improve inter-city connectivity in the country. It will be interesting to watch residential property price movements in the coming years.

LEGAL MATTERS

GET THE PAPERWORK DONE

Are you planning to move into your own home? Here are some documents you must ensure are in order:

Generally Festival seasons are considered auspicious for any new venture. This includes purchase of property as well as moving in. Many people, who have bought property or are in the final stages of completing the purchase, try to move in around this time. It is expected that this will bring in prosperity and luck. While planning to move into your new home, you should ensure that the paperwork is completed and you have all the necessary documents originals plus photocopies – ready.

SOME OF THESE MAJOR DOCUMENTS ARE:

AGREEMENT TO SELL:

This is basically an agreement between a buyer and seller containing the terms of sale. This is important if the sale deed is note executed. It is not required to be registered. It can be used in a court in case of dispute.

SALE DEED:

This is by far the most important document in a property purchase transaction. The sale deed is executed by a buyer and seller. It confirms transfer of property. The deed is executed on stamp paper, after paying stamp duty as per the State's laws. A sale deed is required to be registered in the office of the registrar.

ALLOTMENT LETTER, POSSESSION CERTIFICATE:
An allotment letter is normally issued by the builder or the development authority. It contains details of allotment of property.

The seller should issue a possession certificate to you. This confirms that the full possession of the property has been passed on to you and the seller has no further rights or interests in the property.

LATEST TAX PAID RECEIPT:
This is an important document. You should ask for the latest municipal tax paid receipt and ensure that there are no dues. In case there are some dues on the property, you will be liable to pay them at a later point in time. Also, you will not be able to get the property mutated in your name till the dues are cleared.

LATEST MUTATION LETTER:
In case of a pre-owned you should ask for the latest mutation letter of the municipal authority. This letter shows in whose name the property is in the municipal records.

ENCUMBRANCE CERTIFICATE:
Encumbrance Certificate is to be obtained, latest one, from the Registrar's office or Sub-Registrar's office pertaining the ownership of the land owner or the building owner, by paying the requisite fee to the Registrar/Sub-Registrar office for this certificate purpose.

LATEST BILLS PAID:
You should ask the seller to provide up-to-date electricity bill paid receipt till the time of sale of property. Any due should be paid by the seller, or else you will become liable for it. Same is the case with water bill.

NO OBJECTION CERTIFICATE:
It is advisable to take a **NO OBJECTION** from the seller for the purpose of transfer of electricity connection, water connection and mutation in the municipal records.

RECEIPT FOR SALE AMOUNT:
The seller should provide a receipt for the full amount received as consideration for the sale of property, containing complete details of bank, cheque number, date and amount. It should be duly signed.

SANCTIONED BUILDING PLAN, SHARE CERTIFICATE:
The sanctioned plan is important to ensure that the building has been constructed in compliance with the legal provisions and there are no violations. In case of a society, you

need to get the share certificate from the seller in original showing the seller's membership.

NEVER TOO LATE TO BUY IN THE FESTIVE SEASON.

If you have not been able to complete the registration process in time to move in this festive season, there is another option. Pay a token advance now and complete the buying process later. Here are some factors you need to take into account while doing so.

Apart from being an auspicious occasion, there are a number of festive offers floated by developers as well as banks that make the bargains better.

> **IF YOU ARE PLANNING TO INITIATE THE PROCESS OF ACQUIRING A HOME NOW, BEGIN BY ENSURING THE INITIAL DOCUMENATION IS IN PLACE. YOU CAN ALSO GET AN IN-PRINCIPAL APPROVAL FROM A BANK TO MAKE THE PROCESS OF MAILING A LOAN LATER EASIER.**

Always, the purchase of a property is a major decision. Although one may have planned for it in advance, it still takes time to complete the process. A property purchase process is lengthy as there are many formalities to be taken care of. Also, despite being prepared, there are many formalities that can be completed only after the property has been finalized.

Most prospective home-buyers like to complete the property purchase process during the festive period. Those who are not in a position to complete the process and move in during the festive season have an option too.

A practical option that many homebuyers opt for is short-listing a property that meets their requirements and budget, and paying a token amount to the seller during this period. This way, there actually reserves the property. This is a relatively easier process where you can just pay a nominal mutually-agreed advance amount to the seller. This doesn't take much time either, and you would have completed the formality of initiating the purchase during the festive period.

Once this is done, you can concentrate on the other formalities later.

TITLE CHECK

This is a very important step. It needs to be ensured that the title of the property is clear and marketable, and there are no legal encumbrances on it. This is best done by a lawyer.

HOME LOAN

The next step is to make pans to avail a bank loan. In case you have a pre-approval from a bank already, you need to inform the bank about the property purchase, the final price, required loan amount, details of the seller, likely date of registration, etc.

The bank will also get a proper legal due diligence and valuation done on the property before disbursing the loan. This takes around a week.

DOCUMENTATION

The legal documents need to be drafted. These include the agreement to sell and sale deed. The agreement to sell needs to be signed by both parties at the time of paying the token advance to the seller. This agreement contains the broad terms of sale, property details, names of the parties, sale consideration, time-frame for payment etc. This may take 2-3 days.

The sale deed needs to be drafted too. This is the proof of ownership of property. It will contain the complete details of past ownership of the property as well as other details as contained in the agreement to sell. This may take 2-3 days also.

DOWN PAYMENT

Apart from the bank loan, you need to generate your own share of the finance – the down payment (also known as margin money). This is usually 20-25 percent of the registration value. You can generate this amount by encashing some fixed deposits, selling some shares etc.

These steps can be completed concurrently as well.

PROCESS OF REGISTRATION

On the appointed date, the buyer has to pay the sale amount to the seller. The seller and buyer need to go the registrar's office along with the sale deed. An ID proof and witnesses are needed too. The sale deed is then registered in the office of the registrar.

The registered sale deed can be collected after a few days from the registrar's office. This then completes the sale and registration process.

======

FROM CITY OF PEARS TO AN I.T. HUB

Hyderabad is 425 Today.
History buffs hail iconic city

The historic Hyderabad city, built by Muhammad Quli Qutb, fifth ruler of the Qutb Shahi dynasty, turns 425. The picturesque city, a successor to over-crowded Golconda fort, grew in the last four centuries from a city of minarets, pearls, diamonds, lakes, architectural beauty, art and culture into a vibrant metropolis and international I-T hub.

It hasn't lost its cosmopolitan "Ganga Jamuna tehzeeb", the taste of the famed biryani, spicy slang or tasty Gandipet ka paani (sweet water of Osmansagar), though "adaab" has paved the way for "Hi".

While the Telangana State Government doesn't find it fit to celebrate the occasion for reasons unknown, the Deccan Heritage Trust is organizing an exhibition of vintage photographs of Charminar and Mahaboob Ali Pasha, the sixth Nizam, at Urdu Hall in Himayatnagar.

Paigah Family scion M.A. Kaiz Khan summed up Hyderabad on its 425th birth anniversary: "From a very quiet, peaceful city with culture and tradition, Hyderabad has grown into a vibrant metro. In the process it lost a bit of tradition and culture. Heritage has taken a beating. Yet it is the most successful city where people love to live".

Quli Qutb Shah (1580-1612) laid the foundation for Hyderabad with Charmina (1591-1592) followed by the Badshahi Ashoorkhana in 1593-1594 to house the Alam or replicas of the banner carried by Imam Hussain at Karbala and Darulshifa, Asia's first Unani and Ayurveda hospital in 1595; all in the walled city of Hyderabad.

There was no looking back.

The city grew and grew over the last four centuries especially during the rule of Mir Osman Ali Khan, Nizam VII and thereafter.

It's a great city to live. It has unparalleled culture that bonds people irrespective of caste, creed and color.

Hyderabad is situated on a hilly terrain around artificial lakes, including the Hussainsagar.

In 1724, Mughal viceroy Asif Jah I declared sovereignty and set up his own Nizam dynasty. Nizam's dominion became a princely state during British Raj, and remained so for 150 years, with the city serving as sits capital. Relics of Qutb Shahi and Nizams rule are visible even today.

Hyderabad city was the capital of Hyderabad State. It was the capital of Andhra Pradesh after joining Indian Union in 1948 and is now joint capital for 10 years for Telangana and Andhra Pradesh.

THE RAILWAY STABE [1875-1908] HELPED CEMENT THE WIN CITIES, NEW INDUSTRIES BECAME NUCLEI OF NEW SETLEMENTS.

CITY GREW IN 6 PHASES

How did Hyderabad and Secunderabad grow into a burgeoning metropolis? Historian D.M. Wagh, writing on "Towns and Cities of the Deccan" and quoting Shah Manzsur Alam's "Hyderabad and Secunderabad (Twin Cities) 1965," says the development of Hyderabad-Secunderabad took place in six historical stages.

First, the twin city stage (1591-1687) when the city was planned in a grid pattern and became a commercial metropolis of the Golconda kingdom.

Second, the transitional stage (1591-1687) when the seat of authority was shifted to Hyderabad from Aurangabad. The city wall was completed in 1740.

Third, early Asaf Jahi phase (1725-1799) when there was great economic stress and strain on Hyderabad as Aurangabad was still the capital and many wealthy land holders migrated. The city began growing in 1763 when the Nizam shifted to the city.

Fourth, the subsidiary alliance with British was made in 1798. British cantonment was formed in the north (Secunderabad). Golconda, the twin city of Hyderabad, was replaced with Secunderabad.

Fifth, the railway stage (1875-1908) which helped cement twin cities further, new industries cropped up and became nuclei of new settlement.

Sixth, the stage (from 1908), following the catastrophic floods which led to internal reorganization.

Since then, a new city has come up in the form of Cyberabad which is located cheek by jowl with Hyderabad.

In a lifespan of 357 years from 1591 to 1948, Hyderabad has undergone extensive metamorphosis owing to changing historical, political, economic forces. Its population varied from 150,000 (a rough estimate by the British Resident) in 1839 to 860,000 in 1951.

Since 1901, the population of the city increased more through influx of immigrants than by any other cause – 200,000 immigrants during 1901 to 1941 and from 64,000 in 1941 to 200,000 in 1951.

NEW DISTRICTS AND GROWTH

The new district formation is likely to bring into focus the developmental activity in each of them, and also benefit Hyderabad (Telangana State-India)

With the formation of new districts, there is likely impact on real estate. But perhaps just now. As the districts have just been formed (31 Districts in Telangana State of India) appreciation of rental values are a result of demand and supply and this can happen only after development activity starts. So, the impact will not be immediate, it has been observed by Real Estate Dealers and Observers & Public.

The formation of these new districts is likely to benefit the real estate development of Hyderabad as well. Each district will have a population of 3.4 to 4 lakh. It will help in implementation of government schemes and projects such as infrastructure, irrigation, transport and so on. This in turn, will positively impact the economy of the new districts which is likely to create an inflow of project for Hyderabad's businesses. It will definitely compliment Hyderabad's real estate development. Also, the development in the new districts will curtail migration of people to Hyderabad, balancing Hyderabad population.

What are the likely drivers of growth? There are chances that the technology developments which are now focused in Nanakramguda, Adibatla and Hyderabad-Warrangal corridor may expand within these existing locations or corridors for the time being, as businesses may want to stay in the Hyderabad district, unless the government promotes such de elopements in the newly formed districts Otherwise, most of the newly formed districts have either manufacturing setups or natural mineral resources which can explored and developed further for their economic development. Most districts are likely to promote their local arts and crafts for tourism development initially and slowly start moving into sectors such as agro-industries and manufacturing which can be done with local resources.

District	Resource	Development Potential
Mancherial	River Godavari, Cement Factories, unused airstrip and power plants manufacturing	River front development for tourism, manufacturing
Nirmal	Toy making and existing forts	Art tourism and historical tourism

Warrangal Urban	IT and Colleges	Education and IT sector development
Suryapet Nalgonda Medak	Existing manufacturing hub	Manufacturing sector development
Karimnagar	Granite quarries	Manufacturing sector development

BUILDERS ARE ALL EARS TO THE NEW MASTER PLAN

Builders see great opportunity and also warn of the need for flawless implementation for success.

The expansion and development of the city to the extent the plan promises, has all the potential to give the Real Estate business in the city a tremendous boost.

The grand plans of the HYDERABAD METRO DEVELOPMET AUTHORITY (HMDA) for the future expansion of the city have excited citizens. Realtors and developers seem to have great hopes from the master plan as well. The expansion and development of the city to the extent the plan promises has all the potential to give the real estate business in the city a tremendous boost.

Talking about the positive developments that the plan can bring about "The HMDA master plan amalgamates the earlier 5 existing master plans and comes out with a comprehensive plan which gives clarity on zoning regulations, fee structures etc. This will help the builders and layout developers to properly plan their projects. Development of land will only be done by licensed developers who are professional and more accountable. Layouts will be done in compliance with all regulatory measures. We are already seeking a boom in the real estate and the new master plan will act as an accelerator and take Hyderabad to the next level and make it a truly global city"

A planned city will also bring about added advantages. "Because of a proper master plan the real estate will definitely get a boost and the developers will know where the development and infrastructure will come and there they can venture accordingly to make offices or residence as per the zoning. Property prices will go up with the upcoming development. A planned city also attracts foreign investments and becomes a hub of sorts. It gets spoken internationally."

However, the glorious picture of the city that the master plans projects has its own consequences. One can challenge the flexibility of building options. "Suppose someone wants to develop a residential project in an area that has been demarcated as an industrial or office zone, he would not be able to do it due to zoning restrictions."

Most of the land listed in the plan is under agricultural land. Turning that into non-agricultural land for residential or commercial use would be difficult as this procedure has not seen much success rate in the last couple of years."

One puts in a warning note – "The plan is so huge in nature that it has to be flawless or else it can affect the development and in turn the economy of the state. Instead of considering only the geographical positioning the authorities should also take the market force there into consideration If other infrastructure like good connectivity is not present, then people will not go and live there. So, if the plan is not absolutely free of loopholes, it cannot help the real estate or anybody for that matter.

The following are the places at Hyderabad (Telangana State) INDIA where the Real Estate boom is in full swing and is in much demand, because of its close proximity to all the business sectors including IT/ITeS and other manufacturing, industrial and Trade fields both IT and Non-IT sector. Therefore, it is the need of hour for any person to go in for Land procurement or for Flat purchase, may be 1/2/3/4/5 BHK Houses. It is worth purchasing the property in these areas, as per the effective survey conducted. Now, presently, all the prices of land and flats are within the reach of any buyer (middle class and upper middle-class people) and higher standard of people). In future, it may be difficult for common people to purchase land or flats in these areas. This is the right opportunity for people who are interested to go in for Property.

PEOPLE ARE MOVING TO THE WESTERN QUADRANT NOT ONLY BECAUSE OF PROFESSIONAL REASONS, BUT ALSO BECAUSE IT IS PERCEIVED TO BE THE MOST HAPPENING AREA IN THE CITY MOST OF THE BIG CITY EVENTS HAPPEN IN THE AREA, AND YOUNG PEOPLE WHO HAVE GROWN UP IN HYDERABAD, AND LIVE IN OTHER AREAS, ALSO WISH TO MOVE THERE. THIS STRONG DEMAND HAS A HELPED RENTAL VALUATIONS RISE.

- DESTINATION KUKATPALLY
- DESTINATION MANIKONDA
- DESTINATION UPPAL
- DESTINATION PUPPALAGUDA – NARSINGI
- DESTINATION KHAJA GUDA
- DESTINATION FINANCIAL DISTRICT
- DESTINATION BACHUPALLY
- DESTINATION MADHAPUR
- DESTINATION GACHIBOWLI
- DESTINATION MIYAPUR
- DESTINATION BALANAGAR
- DESTINATION NALLAGNDLA
- DESTINATION NARSINGI
- DESTINATION KONDAPUR
- DESTINATION L B NAGAR
- DESTINATION KOMPALLY
- DESTINATION CHANDA NAGAR
- DESTINATION EAST MAREDPALLY
- DESTINATION LINGAMPALLY
- DESTINATION NALLAGANDLA
- DESTUBATUIB NAGOLE
- DESTINATION VANASTHALIPURAM
- DESTINATION ADIBATLA
- DESTINATION HAYAT NAGAR
- DESTINATION RAJENDRA NAGAR

(Rates vary, as per prevailing land and flat costs)

REAL TRENDS;

DESTINATION KUKATPALLY

(HYDERABAD-TELANGANA STATE-INDIA)

Kukatpally is a well-developed locality with proximity to Hitec City, Madhapur and L&T Info city. The area enjoys bus and rail connectivity through TSRTC and Hitech City MMTS station. The locality witnessed a slight increase in the average property rates by 1% in April-June 2016 quarter.

Kukatpally is a very good location. It is just minutes away from Hitech City and Kondapur. It is near D-Mart Schools, Colleges, Markets, shopping malls and theatres. It has good connectivity through roads with the rest of the city.

Kukatpally is a prime location. It is centrally and strategically located to important places in Hyderabad West region. It has good Schools, Hospitals, and Restaurants in this region. It is just 800 meters from Mumbai Highway and Metro Station.

Kukatpally is a well-developed residential location. It is well connected by trains, buses and public transports. Vegetable markets, shops, hotels, hospitals, banks, super markets are available in this locality. Families prefer this locality.

Kukatpally is one of the most happening places in Hyderabad at the moment. This extends the realty value of **Kukatpally** and makes it worth the investment.

Kukatpally, within a short span of time has found a place in the favorite list for residential and commercial destinations in Hyderabad (Telangana State-India). The expansion of IT and ITeS sectors has generated an influx of employers to the area and this in turn has increased the demand for residential establishments. Slowly and steadily, the area has now been transformed to a commercial, residential and education hub providing the residents with the comfort of amenities, connectivity and proximity.

Kukatpally, is situated on the north-western part of the city of Hyderabad, in the Ranga Reddy district. The area lies to the east of **Hafeezpet** and to the north of **Kothaguda, Hitech City** and **Madhapur.** With an extensive road network, **Kukatpally** is connected with all the major localities. The main bus stops are the **Kukatpally** bus stop and the KPHB bus stop.

The Mumbai Highway runs almost through the center of this locality, and connects it to places like **Ameerpet, Banjara Hills, Moosapet** and **Miyapur.**

The area is quite close to the MMTS run stations of **Hitech City, Borabanda and Bharatnagar, Secunderabad, Nampally** and **Begumpet** are the major railway stations nearby. "I am very peculiar about the connectivity when it comes to buying a house as I am ambitious to buy an independent house or a 3/4BHK Flat, if the God wishes me to have. How comfortable, big or affordable the house is, if there are no proper facilities for commutation, it is difficult. I believe public transportation always has an upper hand to private transportation.

Kukatpally does not trouble us with transportation issues. There are a number of TSRTC buses, private buses, cabs and auto rickshaws plying in the area," This is personal view, because I have been residing in this area in a rental house all these years.

The residential projects in **Kukatpally** vary across a wide range of budgets. Starting from posh luxury villas to budget apartments, and gated townships, there are plenty of options for anyone who wants to buy a house here. The locality witnessed a slight increase in the average property rates by 1% in April 2016 to June 2016 quarter. For residential houses, the average rate card per square feet is across a wide range of budgets. Starting from posh luxury villas to budget apartments, and gated townships, there are plenty of options for anyone who wants to buy a house here. The locality witnessed a slight increase in the average property rates by 1% in April 2016 to June 2016 quarter.

For residential houses, the average rate card per square feet is INR 4,000, ranging between INR 3500 and 5000. For residential plots, the average rate per square yard is Rs. 25,000. The just average price for l BHK and 2 BHK apartments ranges from INR 7,000 to 15,000 and INR 15,000 to INR 30,000 respectively. For 3 BHK apartments, the price starts from INR 20,000 and it can go up to even INR 40,000. This is only in KPHB Phases 1, 2, 3,4,5,67,8 and 9 only.

If it is at **Hitech City, Madhapur, Kondapur, Manikonda** areas, the prices are entirely different and on higher side. Generally, normal and average person cannot afford to purchase houses here in these areas.

Kukatpally is an ideal residential area. With the presence of commendable social infrastructure, many families prefer **Kukatpally** for their home. It has plenty of good schools, educational institutions and hospitals. The area is segmented into many residential colonies; popular among them are **Kukatpally Housing Board colony (KPHB), Bhagya Nagar colony, Vasanth Naga colony** and many more.

Along with the commercial development, the construction of the **Kukatpally Housing Board** colony has also played a major role I the growth of this locality. This colony, which is one of the best developed residential colonies in Telangana has triggered a huge surge of buyers flocking to this area. The demand for other residential projects around the colony also increased, because of the overall development in physical and social infrastructure in **Kukatpally.**

Kukatpally is also known as the shopping Centre of Hyderabad. There are a number of branded stores, factory outlets, malls and show rooms in here. My friends, staying in different area of **Hyderabad** usually come over to **Kukatpally** and we do the shopping together. **Kukatpally** offers many hang out places to enjoy our week-ends.

MY ADVICE IS THAT IF WE PURCHASE A SIZEABLE LAND IN MADHAPUR OR HITECH CITY OR AT MANIKONDA OR AT KONDAPUR AREAS (Square Yards 800 - 1200 = Two (2) Plots initially, and construct 5 Story Apartments with Flats of 2/3/4 BHK) and if we construct with our own funds, the rents deriving out of these Flats will be a recurring amount for over 60-70 years.

This is a very good profitable venture.

If you can invest into this type venture, really, it is an achievement for us.

I will look-after everything regarding Plan Approvals, Material Procurement, Construction, Bricks, Cement, Steel, Sand, Tiles/Marble Flooring, Lappam finishing, Painting, Grills, doors Wardrobes, windows, drainage system, Water connection, Bore Machine, underground sumps, wood work, plumbing works, Electricity works connections, Lift arrangement, Generator arrangement etc. etc.

You have to Bell the Cat and arrange for this big venture. This venture will be completed in 2-3 years' time.

THIS IS A WORTHY VENTURE.

REAL TRENDS

DESTINATION MANIKONDA

AREA [NEAR HITEC CITY

Manikonda is one of the preferred areas for residential and commercial development as it holds a lot of scope for growth.

MANIKONDA SNAPSHOT

Manikonda is rapidly growing commercial-cum-residential area. Lanco Hills project deserves a mention. It includes residential, commercial and IT SEZ.

In 2013 the state's Lokayukta asked buyers to exercise caution as apartments might be illegal and permission is only to construct ground plus two floors.

RESUDEBT'S REVIEW

Manikonda is good for investment as I is a very peaceful with all the required facilities. Roads are a least 40 ft wide. It is well-connected to schools, markets, hospitals, banks and ATMs.

Manikonda is connected to primary & idle level schools and few nursing homes, hospitals and market and shopping complex. RTC and auto stand enable commuters to access IT Corridors like Gachibowli and Madhapur.

Manikonda is a fantastic locality and excellent facilities which has resulted in great demand within a few years. Excellent for people of all ages. Lot of schools and colleges nearby and temples for devotees. Very quiet and peaceful environment.

Manikonda with its booming developmental activities is emerging as one of the fastest growing suburbs and one of the most sought-after destinations for commercial and residential developments. The suburb with its presence of leading software Company headquarters and high-rise residential township is already among the top posh areas of the city. The presence of IT companies in Manikonda itself and proximity to the IT/ITeS hubs of Gachibowli and Madhapur has led to the flourishing of residential and commercial real estate here.

The Lanco Hills, Manikonda Cheruvu Lake, and Shaikpet Dargah, Chitrapuri Colony residential layout for Telugu cinema workers are some famous landmarks of the area. Manikonda has many residential colonies such as Panchvati colony, Bhagyalatha colony, Laxmi Nagar colony, etc. Gachibowli has given mileage to the lots of areas within the radius of few kilometers. Manikoda is one example. The area is very close to the Outer Ring Road and is well connected to other parts of the city. This has attracted various investors to the area.

TSRTS buses regularly ply on the roads here. There are a number of autos and shared auto available for short distance communication. The nearest MMTS station is in Hi The city, which is at a distance of 10 kms, Rajiv Gandhi International Airport (RGIA) is at a distance of 28 kms. Secunderabad Railway Station is 18 kms away, while Jubilee Bus Station is at a distance of 19kms. Mahatma Gandhi Bus Station is 19 kms. Away. Commutation is never a problem for the residents here. We have buses, autos and shared autos and cabs, plying in the area.

The social infrastructure is keeping good pace with the real estate development in Manikonda. There are many shops and restaurants on Manikonda main road. Malls and shopping centers n the nearby areas of Madhapur and Kukatpally serve all the shopping and entertainment need of the residents in Manikonda. There are international schools and hospitals as well in the area. Manikonda is connected to primary and middle level schools and few nursing homes, hospitals and market and shopping complex. RTC and auto stand enable commuters to access IT Corridors like Gachibowli and Madhapur.

Manikonda has a lot of housing options from gated communities to stand along apartment buildings. The area has good housing options in the affordable rate. While 2 nd 3 BHK apartments are more in demand, gated community villas too is a sought after housing option here.

Manikonda is a rapidly growing commercial-cum-residential area sharing neighborhood with localities such as Gachibowli, Jubilee Hills and Kondapur. It saw an increase in the average property value by 7.5% (April-June Quarter 2016). Manikonda offers a decent living environment.

Manikonda is surrounded by 3 nationalized banks and 2 international schools. It is also close to schools, hospitals, colleges and super markets. It is well-connected to roads.

REAL TRENDS

DESTINATION UPPAL

- Uppal is known as a well-developed part of Hyderabad with presence of good social infrastructure and IT companies. The locality has immense potential which has been indicated by its increasing renal yield.

- The locality is expected more new developments owing to the commencement of work of Metro. Uppal has a metro station of its own which is expected to be functional anytime soon.

RESIDENT'S VIEW

- Uppal is a very prime location in Hyderabad. It is well-connected by trains, buses and public transports. All the facilities like schools, malls, markets, banks and ATMs are available. Transport facility is also good here.

- Uppal is a very calm and peaceful location. It is near to banks, schools and hospitals within close proximity shopping cenger. Rythu Bazar, public transport, Park Avenue, Plantation, bus stop and ATMs close by. Closeness to National Highway 65 is an added bonus.

- Uppal is very nice locality. It is great place for quality lifestyle. It is near several every day necessities such as education hub, newly constructed shopping mall, police station, schools and colleges.

UPPAL and the surrounding villages are seeing fast-paced growth and development with increasing number of residential and commercial establishments

Uppal is one of the growing suburbs in Hyderabad. It is located in the GHMC area, to the east of Hyderabad city on National Highway 163 to Bhongir town and Northern bank of River Musi. This area is a chosen location for real estate investors because of its better connectivity and reachable amenities. Not only residential but also commercial establishments are on the rise in the area. The area houses a number of MNCs, Genpact and Infosys to name a few and this, in turn, is giving a boost to Uppal's real estate market.

Despite being the centre of fast-paced development, the area also provides a fresh and clean atmosphere with its lush greenery.

Along with all these facilities, metro connectivity is one boon for the area which gives Uppal real estate, the biggest advantage. Given the connectivity boosted by metro rail, the locality in the eastern part of the city is poised for further development. There has been a price surge in the area even before construction of metro rail was undertaken.

Areas near Uppal offer a calm, green and pollution-free environment with good connectivity to other parts of the city. Uppal is well connected to Ghatkesar and Bhongir town. Shamshabad airport is 45 minutes' drive from Uppal while Imliban bus stand is 9 km away. Secunderabad railway station is at a distance of 12 km from the area. The area is well connected with TSRTC buses and autos. So commutation cannot be a problem in this area.

Apart from IT and ITeS companies, there are many international schools, colleges and hospitals forming the areas social fabric. The Hyderabad Public School, Little Flower Junior College, Rajiv Gandhi International Cricket Stadium, National Geophysical Research Institute, CCMB, National Institute of Nutrition, National Mineral Development Corporation is few places of interest in Uppal. The area is excellent for families.

The area also has good schools and hospitals nearby. The locality houses a few big names like Reliance Trends, D Mart, Decathlon, along with a number of supermarkets and shops.

Affordability is another factor which is making Uppal, a better residential option. The rate card is very affordable. The average rental for a 1 BHK apartment comes between Rs. 4000 and Rs. 8000. For 2 BHK and 3 BHK, the rate card is between Rs. 9000to Rs. 16,000 and Rs. 12,500 to Rs. 25,000 respectively. There are also open plots available for investment in the area, especially near the Outer Ring Road (ORR).

UPPAL and the surrounding villages are seeing fast-paced growth and development with increasing number of residential and commercial establishments.

UPPAL is one of the growing suburbs in Hyderabad. It is located in the GHMC area, to the east of Hyderabad city on National Highway 163 to Bhongir town and Northern bank of River Musi. This area is a chosen location for real estate investors because of its better connectivity and reachable amenities. Not only residential but also commercial establishments are on the rise in the area. The area houses a number of MNCs, Genpact and Infosys to name a few and this, in turn, is giving a boost to Uppal's real estate market. Despite being the center of fast-paced development, the area also provides a fresh and clean atmosphere with its lush greenery.

Along with all these facilities, metro connectivity is one boon for the area which gives UPPAL real estate, the biggest advantage. Given the connectivity boosted by metro rail, the locality in the eastern part of the city is poised for further development.

"There has been a price surge in the area even before construction of metro rail was undertaken", as I have been observing the real estate trends of marketing and price rise.

Areas near UPPAL offer a calm, green and pollution-free environment with good connectivity to other parts of the city. UPPAL is well connected to Ghatkesar and Bhongir town. Shamshabad airport is 45 minutes' drive from UPPAL while Mahatma Gandhi Bus Station is 9 KM away. Secunderabad Railway Station is at a distance of 12 KM from the area. "The area is well connected with TSRTC BUSES and Autos. So, communication cannot be a problem in this area.

This I have been observing for the last 20-25 years. I worked in this Uppal area at Central Government for four (4) years during 1969-73 at which time there was nothing in this area except a single road and a jungle type look-alike area.

Apart from IT and ITeS companies, there are many international schools, colleges and hospitals forming the area's social fabric. The Hyderabad Pubic School, Little Flower Junior College, Rajiv Gandhi International Cricket Stadium, National Geophysical Research Institute, CCMB, National Institute of Nutrition, National Mineral Development Corporation are few places of interest in UPPAL.

The area is excellent for families. The previous places we lived in were much cluttered. It is a clean and safe locality to live.

This is my observation and knowledge on Real Estate.

The area also has good schools and hospitals nearby. The locality houses a few big names like Reliance Trends, D-Mart, Decathlon, along with a number of super markets and shops.

Affordability is another factor which is making UPPAL, a better residential option. The rate card is very affordable. The average rental for a 1 BHK apartment comes between INR 5,000 to INR 10,000. For 2 BHK and 3 BHK, the rate card is between INR 10,000 to INR 15,000 and INR 16000 to INR 25,000 respectively.

There are also open plots available for investment in the area, especially near the Outer Ring Road (ORR).

REAL TRENDS:

DESTINATION PUPPALAGUDA – NARSINGI

HERE'S WHY?

OWING TO THE NEW EMPLOYMENT ARENAS, HOUSING DEMAND IN WEST HYDERABAD MAY GROW. HOWEVER, CONSIDERING THE PRICE ADVANTAGE, THE PUPPALGUDA-NARSINGI CLUSTER IS LIKELY TO BENEFIT,

Along with affordability and connectivity, the location and proximity are significant factors one should consider while investing.

As a rule of thumb, never compromise on the location of your house, if you can afford to. Experts believe that a house in close proximity to business districts, hospitals and schools, shopping complexes helps in getting a better return on investment. If you are looking at end use, these act as convenience quotients. Simply put, check how accessible your location is.

The smoother the physical and social infrastructure around, the more it is worth. With time, such ideal, central locations may be saturated and you would need to look at the next best alternative. In Hyderabad check out the **PUPPAGUDA – NARSINGI STRETCH THAT IS BEING TOUTED AS A STRATEGIC INVESTMENT DESTINATION.**

If you cannot afford HITEC City or Gachibowli, the central locations to have a house in and are looking at an affordable best, this corridor, to the south of the financial district is a location with potential.

While the office market isn't mature here yet, it has the benefit of being simply 30 minutes away from the major bulk of business locations such as Gachibowli, HITEC City, Nanakramguda, Raidurgam, Kondapur and Kothaguda. Over the next five years, an added 10 million square feet of office spaceis expected. A recent Knight Frank Report states that this means an incremental employment for about 1,25,000 employees. Easy to assume that when jobs are created, housing demanded goes up.

WHAT ABOUT INFRASTRUCTURE?

Although well connected to HITEC City via the Lanco Hills Road and the main road, the route via the Outer Ring Road is an alternative but in dire need of repair. However, as a respite is the under construction four lane road that will connect the region directly to the ORR. Once complete, you can expect the usually half an hour's journey down to 15 minutes.

The Hyderabad Metropolitan Water Supply and Sewerage Board have also undertaken the initiative to provide piped water supply to **PUPPALAGUDA GRAM PANCHAYAT.** This is expected to make residential inventory in the area more favorable. As buyers, one wouldn't need to go too far for malls, hospitals, schools or the international airport. Further, improving the connectivity is the flyover that will connect the area to Old Mumbai Highway.

PRICING

Owing to the new employment arenas, housing demand in West Hyderabad may grow. However, considering the price advantage, the **PUPPALAGUDA-NARSINGI** cluster is likely to benefit. While prices in the western market is in the range of INR 4500 – INR 7000 per sq.ft, that in this area is mostly within
4000 per sq.ft. It makes sense to be considering residential options along these newly evolving localities where you will have the early bird advantage of price benefits, less traffic, more space and a scope of appreciation in the mid to long run.

This I have observed through various TV channel news and also read in various Daily News Papers.

At this price, the area is just a 30-minute drive from **KONDAPUR.**

REAL TRENDS:

DESTINATION KHAJA GUDA

IT IS A GOOD INVESTMENT OPTION

THE OUTER RING ROAD [ORR] CONNECT AND SOCIAL INFRASTRUCTURE MAKE THE AREA A STRONG AND VIABLE LONG-TERM INVESTMENT

NEHRU OUTER RING ROAD IS CONNECTED WITH THE GACHIBOWLI FLYOVER AND OLD MUMBAI HIGHWAY THAT CONNECTS KHAJA GUDA WITH GACHIBOWLI, NANAKRAM GUDA AND MANY OTHER SIGNIFICANT PARTS OF THE CITY.

KHAJA GUDA on Outer Ring Road enjoys special preference by both developers and buyers. The reason is not just its strategic location, but also guaranteed Return on Investment (ROI) on properties housed in this locality. Its price history since the last six (6) months has been impressive and has registered an increase by 1.7 percent as per Magic bricks research.

Khaja Guda shares its border with Nehru Outer Ring Road. Its popularity amongst consumers can be because of its nearness to the IT hubs of Financial District and Hitec City, both located within 5 to 7 km radius.

One builder staff said, "Not only does the locality have close proximity to the IT/ITeS hubs, but another positive aspect could be the new developments coming along in the locality, Government efforts to improve its connectivity to Outer Ring Road has further captured the attention of buyers and developers".

INCREASING PROPERTY VALUES:

Khaja Guda witnessed a price rise of 1.7 per cent in the April – June 2016 quarter. In the April – June 2015 quarter the average price of apartment was INR 4,500 per sq. ft which increased to INR 4, 800 per sq. ft in the same quarter of 2016.

CONNECTED AND DEVELOPED:

Khaja Guda being one of the localities along the ORR, is well-connected to the Financial District. Its growth potential is immense as prime areas such as **MANIKONDA AND HITEC CITY are also linked through the ORR.**

Some major international schools are within the vicinity. The airport is only a couple of minutes' drive away. The IT hub of Hitec City has garnered attention of many IT professionals who would like to stay close to their work spaces. ORR stretch in Khaja Guda being the closest, within 3-km distance, tops buyer's preference charts.

Nehru Outer Ring Road is connected with the Gachibowli Flyover and Old Mumbai Highway that connects Khaja Guda with Gachibowli, Anakra Guda and many other significant parts of the city. Telangana State Road Transport Corporation (TSRTC) offers public mode of transport.

INVESTING IN KHAJA GUDA:

If one is a first-time buyer, Khaja Guda will not disappoint you. The locality offers both under-construction and ready-to-move-in properties. Popular housing formats are 2, 3, and 4 BHK units.

Under construction properties can be priced fro INR 35 lakh to INR 2 crore and above. Read-to-move in units are priced up to INR 3 crore depending upon its size and amenities.

In terms of amenities, residential projects offer facilities keeping in mind the needs and requirements of professionals, families, kids and elderly citizens. New constructions offer modern amenities such as parking lot, cafeteria, drinking water, round-the-clock security, bench seating arrangements, club house, water storage, elderly parks, among others.

However, it is advised to check the amenities yourself as every project differs from another. Also, invest in amenities that you will use. Buyers in the past have complained that they pay a hefty annual deposit for the maintenance of facilities that they might use once in a year only.

DESTINATION FINANCIAL DISTRICT REVIEW:

Financial District is close to IT companies. It is surrounded by greenery. All high-end personalities live in the locality. It is very close to international airport. It is a comfortable area to reside for senior citizens.

Financial District is a good location to invest. Major IT companies such as Wipro, Infosys, Msicrosoft, etc have their offices here. It has good connectivity and transport facility. Therefore, owning a house here is profitable.

Financial District is a very good location and is at a walkable distance from the IT companies. It is near shopping complexes, hospitals and famous schools. The social infrastructure is developed and caters well to its residents.

While the Financial District is attracting investors with its developmental activities, housing is attractive too.

Travelling just 10 km from Hitec City takes you to Financial District, the new hub of commercial realty, bustling with development. The Financial District, situated in Gachibowli is spread across 75 acres and is one of the widely chosen localities for residential, commercial and office spaces, considering its close proximity to main centers of Hyderabad.

It is a well-known and developed area of Hyderabad and the locality is about 19 km from Punjagutta and 24 km from Secunderabad. It is very close to technology companies such as Wipro, Miscrosoft and Infosys.

The first phase of the financial district in Hyderabad is also home to business parks, IT/ITES special economic zones, Tishman Speyer, and the Waverock, which houses multinational conglomerates, likes Accenture, TCS, Dupont.

In fact, the area is witnessing wide expansion in terms of infrastructure. The close proximity to Outer Ring Road has attracted investors to this area and is witnessing huge demand from investors. The place is green and clean away from the city pollution, at the same time near the city center. Good connectivity and transport facility is a boon to the area.

If you are looking for a calm and peaceful environment to live in, with basic and urban amenities within reach, the Financial District can be a good option. Added to that, affordability and easy commutation make the locality favorite for residents. Along with apartments and flats, the area also has independent houses, villas and plots unlike other areas in the city. While short listing the places in terms of affordability, proximity and amenities Financial District seemed to be a better option. In terms of neighborhood, cleanliness, safety and connectivity, the local is pretty good than other areas in the city. Financial district is 3 km from the NH19 main road. The Rajiv Gandhi International Airport and the nearest railway station are at a distance of 32 km and 12 km respectively.

The social infrastructure is developed here, and improving rapidly. The area houses a number of good schools, colleges, healthcare centers, restaurants, banks super markets, pharmacy, gym and many more addressing the needs of the residents. After facing stagnancy for a couple of years, the value of the area has revived.

The Financial District is in one way the major activity-oriented locality. It is always buzzing with development. So, investing in such a nucleus cannot be a bad decision. Over the next 10–15-year, real estate development in Hyderabad will be clustered around this area, primarily because of the availability of a large land parcels and availability of amenities.

The locality is also well priced. For multi storied apartments, the average price is Rs. 5,000 per square feet ranging from 4,000 to 5,500 INR per square feet. For a 2BHK flat of 970-1492 sq. feet, the cost ranges between Rs. 36.00 to Rs. 85.00 lakh. The cost of a 3 BHK apartment of size 1200-2500 sq. feet is in the range of Rs. 50.00 to Rs. 1.20 crore. For commercial establishments, the office spaces of size 121-300 sq. feet cost around INR 31 lakhs. Rental housing is difficult to find here. For a 3 BHK apartment the starting rate is INR 20,000 and can evens go up to INR 60,000. Thus, choosing Financial District for your home cannot be a bad decision as it ensures value for money.

======

(Rates vary, as per prevailing land and flat costs)

DESTINATION BACHUPALLY

Bachupally is home to quite a few international schools, colleges and institutions of higher education. Construction of a major university is underway here.

REVIEWS:

The locality has a presence of many IT industries, corporate houses and the Metro connectivity has also made this area a popular residential destination. It has easy access and is well connected to other parts of the city.

Uppal is located in East Hyderabad doing the National Highway-202 and mostly offers independent houses. Average capital value in the area is affordable which makes it easy for people from all budget levels to buy a property of their choice here.

Uppal enjoys equal distance from Hyderabad and Secunderabad. It is 9-10 km from both cities. The area is acceible via the Uppal-Ramanthapur Road and Uppal Main Road, It boasts of developed infrastructure.

Bachupally is a mushrooming suburb on the outskirts of Hyderabad with many apartments, villas and few open plots available. It falls in the Qutbullapur mandal of Ranga Reddy district. The areas proximity to Madhapur and Gachibowli has led to a rapid development of many residential projects. Many residents here are employed in the IT and ITes sector. Bachupally is segmented into many colonies. Most of the apartments are in 2 and 3 & 4 BK format, while villas are built on plots measuring anywhere between 160 sq. yard to 200 sq.yard.

An apartment that is a bit in the interiors will cost INR 2,200 per sq. ft and if one wishes to go for an apartment near the main road then it will cost close to INR 2,600 per sq. ft. An apartment in a gated community with modern amenities such as swimming pool, club houses, etc. will have a price tag of INR 3200 per sq. ft. The starting price of villas here is INR 65 lakhs and will increase depending on the total area of the villa and other built-in amenities. Rentals in Bachupally are fairly affordable. One can find a 2 BHK apartment with a rental tag between INR 5600 to INR 8500 per month. A 3 BHK apartments rental cost will start from Rs. 11,000 per month while a 4 BHK apartment rental will range between INR 15,000 to INR 22,000 per month.

Bachupally crossroads has an RTC bus stop thus connecting the area to other parts of the city. TSRTC buses have regular halts at the bus stop here. There are many shared autos too, available for commutation. Jubilee bus stand is 27 kms away, while Secunderabad Railway Station is at a distance of 29 kms. The nearest MMTS station is in Hafeezpet which is 11 kms away Rajiv Gandhi International Airport is 47 kms away.

The social infrastructure in Bachupally is de eloping rapidly. The area is home to quite a few international schools, colleges and institutions of higher education. Construction of a major university is underway here. Apart from educational institutions, restaurants and hospitals have their presence in the area. For any major shopping requirements, one has to go to Nizamapet or Kukatpally. However, for daily requirements there are many small grocery and daily needs stores in Bachupally itself.

There aren't many open plots available in Bachupally itself. However just 4 kms beyond Bachupally one can find plenty of open plots to choose from The price tag of these open plots is close to INR 5600 per sq. yard. Given the areas proximity to Madhapur and Gachibowlii, investment in open plots here appeal to many. The land rates will rise by 50 per cent here in the next two years.

Whether one chooses to buy a house or live in a rented apartment here, one must be aware of the water shortage that the area experiences. Though there are bore-wells, the water supply is insufficient, forcing residents to rely on water tankers. Also due to the presence of many pharmacy companies in the vicinity, air and land pollution is quite high here. However, there are quite a few Resident Welfare Associations (RWA), which are actively working on improving the conditions.

DESTINATION : MADHAPUR

PROFESSIONALS COMMENTS.

MADHAPUR is a posh location. It has excellent connectivity by buses and metro. It is a 30 minutes' drive from Hyderabad Airport. It is located close to shopping malls, theaters. The social infrastruture is developed.

Madhapur is a premium and decent locality having a good living environment. Schools, banks, ATMs and hospitals are also available near the locality. Transport facility is also good with easy connectivity to other parts of the city.

MADHAPUR is a very good locality to reside. It is well-connected via roads. The existing public transport network is good. Basic amenities such as schools, hospitals, colleges, bank ATMs, and markets are located nearby.

MADHAPUR is at walking distance from Medchal Railway Station (proposed MMTS Hub), Medical Bus Stand, NH-44. It is 25 km from Secunderabad Railway Station; 25 km from Medchal check post to Miyapur Ring Road.

KEY TAKEAWAYS

- Madhapur is a residential-cum-commercial locality which has made its mark by having the highest concentration of IT/ITES companies in Hyderabad, attracting consumers from this profile.
- The nearby localities including Hitec City, Jubliee Hills, Silicon Valley, Vijaya colony, among others.
- Infrastructure developments like Madhapur Main Road widening, proposed metro rail corridor is expected to boost the residential and rental demand further in this locality.
- Apartments in gaged communities and stand alone are preferred by the people for rent.
- Madhapur houses several IT/ITES, BPO and other multinational companies.
- New malls and multiplexes are also coming up in the area, which will give the residents more options for recreation.
- Madhapur is served by the HITEC, MMTS station, which is a kilometer away. APSRTC/TSRTC bus services are also available.
- The area is accessible via the Old Mumbai Highway and the Hitec City Main Road.
- The locality offers apartments, villas, residential houses, residential plots and commercial plots. Most of the apartments available are part of gated communities.

MADHAPUR offers a variety of housing options that cater to different budget ranges and is at the forefront of fast development.

From a suburb, **MADHAPUR** is now one of the hubs which house some of the top IT majors and luxury hotels. With its high concentration of industries and proximity to the IT corridor, the area has gradually developed as a full-fledged residential area and has a number of residential luxury projects and sky touching infrastructure. Hitech city which is situated in the heart of **MADHAPUR** has the highest concentration of IT and ITeS establishments in the city. **MADHAPUR** today is home to large MNCs convention centers.

The area has a rich cosmopolitan flavor with people from different parts of India and different countries working here. "**MADHAPUR** is today one of the best developed areas in the city of terms of commercial as well as residential, offering all the amenities that one could think of.

MADHAPUR is very well connected with other parts of the city. **TSRTC** buses regularly ply to and from the area. Autos and shared autos also are a common mode of transportation. **MMTS** has its station at **MADHAPUR. The Rajiv Gandhi International Airport** is 37 Km away while **Secunderabad Railway Station** is 14 Km away. **Jubilee Bus Station** and **Mahatma Gandhi Bus Stand** are at a distance of 15 Km and 16 Km respectively. Most of the techies prefer **MADHAPUR** as the ideal residential area because of the proximity to their offices and better connectivity.

The area is also rich in cultural and green spaces. The famous art and craft village Shilparamam, an environment for the preservation of traditional craft is located in **MADHAPUR.** The green lungs of the city, Botanical garden is also in **MADHAPUR.** The social infrastructure in **MADHAPUR** is robust and has developed over a period of two decades**. Inorbit mall** services all kinds of shopping and entertainment needs of residents here. The **MADHAPUR** main road has many big and small stores and shopping centers. Big brands, from automobiles to clothing and accessories, have their presence in the area. The area houses a handful of reputed educational institutions and good hospitals.

Whether it's my office, my children's school or my wife's work place, living in **MADHAPUR** has eased our risk of travelling long distances, one medium Trader & Business commented.

Another Businessman comments that "Most of my grocery shopping is done from the super markets which are in a radius of two to three kilometers."

There are many residential colonies in **MADHAPUR, popular among them are Ayyappa Society, Arunodaya colony, Vittal Rao Nagar and Sriram colony.** The capital and the rental values both in **MADHAPUR** area have seen a sharp spike due to due to the constant development and rapid infrastructural growth. Housing options in the area are many, catering to various budget ranges. Hostels, PG accommodation, apartments in l,2 and 3 BHK format and villas in gated communities are all available. The average price value per square feet is INR 5600. For a 1 BHK apartment, the rate is around INR 27 Lakh. For a 2 BHK apartment of 920-1750 square feet, the rate is between INR 33.00 Lakh to INR 75.00 Lakh. For a 3 BHK apartment of 1350-2800 square feet, the rate is between INR 65.00 Lakh to INR 1.50 crore. The rental for apartment varies depending on the amenities and the size of the apartment. For a 1 BHK apartment, the rate is between INR 8000.00 to INR 12000. For a 2 BHK and 3 BHK, the rate ranges between INR 14,000-INR 25,000 and INR 25,000 to even INR 70,000 respectively.

Madhapur, the IT/ITES hub of Hyderabad, offers a variety of housing options that cater to different budget ranges.

Madhapur, the area that brought Hyderabad at the forefront of fast development in the country since the late 90's, is today one of the best developed areas in the city, offering all the amenities that one could think of. With the highest concentration of IT and ITeS companies in the heart of Madhapur that is called the HiTec city, the residential real estate too in the surrounding areas has flourished. Once a non-descript rocky village, Madhapur today is home to large MNCs, five-star hotels, world-class business convention centers along with a number of housing projects and other commercial establishments. Majority of people who live in Madhapur work in the IT and ITeS sectors and also a large chunk of population who work and reside here are from other parts of the country, lending a rich cosmopolitan flavor to the area.

There are many residential colonies in Madhapur, popular among them are Ayyappa Society, Arunodaya colony, Vittal Rao nagar, and Sriram colony. Housing options in the area are galore, catering to various budget ranges. Hostels, PG accommodation, apartments in 1,2 and 3 BHK format and villas in gated communities are all available. The rentals for apartments range between INR 12,000 to 16,000 depending on the amenities and the size of the apartment. Fully furnished apartments will have a rental tag of anywhere between INR 18,000 to INR 22,000. Villas in gated communities will start with a renal tag of INR 40,000 and shoot up to INR 80,000. Considering that many young IT professionals who have just started their career work here, there are many single bedroom apartments and independent houses available, the rental of which start from INR 6,000 and shoot up to INR 12,000 depending on the level of furnishing provided.

Service apartments and suites are also among the various housing options available in Madhapur which primarily cater to executives who need temporary accommodation during their business trip to the city.

Madhapur is very well connected with other parts of the city. TSRTC buses regularly ply to and from the area. Autos and shared autos also are a common mode of transportation for short distance commutation. MMTS has its station at Madhapur. The Rajiv Gandhi International Airport is 37 km away while Jubilee Bus Station is at a distance of 15 km. Secunderabad Railway Station is 14 km away and Mahatma Gandhi Bus Stand is at a distance of 16 km.

The social infrastructure in Madhapur is robust and has developed over a period of two decades. Inorbit mall serves all kinds of shopping and entertainment needs of residents here. The Madhapur main road is dotted with many big and small stores and shopping venders. Big brands, from automobiles to clothing and accessories, have their presence in the area. Five-star hotels along with big and small restaurants are spread across Madhapur. Educational institutions and hospitals too, have their strong presence in the area.

The road infrastructure here has kept pace, especially where large MNCs have set up their offices. Madhapur flyover, 100 feet road and the nearby Outer Ring Road (ORR) sand testimony to this fact. However, roads need to be laid in the interiors of the residential colonies here. Perhaps the only issue that the area faces is that of water shortage. The ground level water in Madhapur I low and also not all residential colonies have municipal water supply. The infrequent municipal water supply which is at times as bad as once a week compels residents here to heavily rely on water tankers.

INVESTMENT IN GACHIBOWLI AND MIYAPUR IS PROFITABLE

Fast fact: **MIYAPUR** is a price sensitive market as compared to **Gachibowli** offering affordable homes. The properties are less expensive.

Location of a residential property is one of the keys deciding factors while short-listing a property. Not only should the house be within the ambit of a developed infrastructure, but it should also have the potential to earn you good earnings in the future.

No one likes to travel a distance to meet their everyday basic needs or live in an environment with no or crumbling infrastructure. It is imperative to have an established social and physical infrastructure to ensure qualitative living standards. This also determines the value of your property. The value of a house in a developed locality is higher.

Gachibowli is a well-established IT/ITes zone. The development of new infrastructure projects and office leasing activity has attracted buyers from other parts of **Hyderabad** and the country. The investment hotspots around **Gachibowli** have ample unsold residential inventory. Most of these residences are priced anywhere between INR 50-90 Lakh.

The hotspots of the area encompass **Manikonda**, **Gachibowli**, **Nallagandla** and other localities. The best part of investing here is that though it is near to the IT/ITeS zone, the properties are yet affordable. Therefore, anyone looking to invest can now buy a cheaper property whose value will increase in years to come, once the infrastructure projects get completed. One of the important projects is the **Hyderabad Metro,** extending its Corridor-3 (**Nagole-Shilparamam)** of Phase-1 that will terminate at **Hitech City.** It is expected that this line will be extended to cover **Gachibowli** as well. If this takes place, property prices will most definitely shoot-up.

Miyapur is a price sensitive market as compared to **Gachibowli** offering affordable homes. The properties are relatively less expensive as compared to localities which are close to IT/ITeS office hubs. The corridor comprises of areas such as **Miyapur, Chandanagar, Nizampet,** and **Bachupally.** These are well-established localities. Despite being a developed area, most of the residential stock offer properties in the INR 25-45 Lakh price bracket.

In line with general market trend, the price level in the corridor has been stagnant for some time. The overall price increment in all these localities near **Miyapur** has been under 10 per cent for the last two years.

The upcoming **Metro** will improve the region's connectivity. Located on National Highway – 9 ensures good road connectivity to other neighboring towns. Infrastructure-wise **Miyapur** looks promising. Making an investment now, will spell profit as property prices are still on the lower side. The best bedroom configuration in **Miyapur** corridor is 2-BHK format both, for buying and renting purpose. Following that is the 3-BHK category.

As **Gachibowli** and **Miyapur** get more popular in the office space market, the overall development will only further improve. Since both of them have affordable properties in their respective markets, putting in money in a suitable property now does make sense.

INVESTMENT HOTSPOTS

WHY SHOULD CONSUMERS REFER TO IT?

Investment Hotspot report gives an in-depth description of the upcoming nodes of the city. The report details the current infrastructure status and future plans of the localities along the stretch. It shares the types of properties available along with their configuration; current property prices and their future prospects. The report will help buyers choose the best sectors for investment.

======

GACHIBOWLI INVESTMENT HOTSPOT

NEW DEVELOPMENT:

NEW DEVELOPMENT IN THE ZONE IS TOWARDS NORTH AND ALONG THE LANGAR HOUSE ROAD WHICH RUNS IN HE EAST-WEST DIRECTION.

RENTAL DEMAND:

RENTAL DEMAND IS OVERWHELMINGLY CONCENTRATED IN GACHIBOWLI AND MANIKONDA BECAUSE THESE ARE CLOSEST TO IT/ITES OFFICE SPACE CLUSGGERS.

Here is an account of how Gachibowli has emerged as an upcoming residential corridor in the Hyderabad city.

CURRENT STATUS OF THE CORRIDOR:

Gachibowli and adjoining Nanakramguda constitutes one of the two major IT/ITes office clusters in the city. Apart from the IT/ITes office buildings, it also has many large captive campuses of leading MNCs in other domains. It is well connected to other parts of Hyderabad through public transport. A branch of the Outer Ring Road (ORR) extends towards Gachibowli and connects to the international airport at Shamshabad and other localities off the ORR.

PRESENT RESIDENTIAL DEVELOPMENT;

Larger and cheater land parcels are available in areas to the north-west and south and consequently, development shifted to these areas. Cheaper land price also translates into relatively less expensive residential units for buyers.

Apartments, residential plots and villa projects are available in Kanchi-Gachibowli Road, Nallagandla Tellapur Road (from Tellapur towards Gachibowli).

Residential development in Manikonda consists mainly of low-rise independent houses. New multi-story apartment projects and gated colonies have come up along the road from Nanakramguda Junction to Khothaguda Cross road. Kokapet can be accessed from ORR at Narsingi Junction. Most of the residential projects in here are located on the Gandipet Road and Golden Mile Road where the Gandipet Road is the main access road from the zone to the ORR. Narsingi is contiguous with Manikonda. New development in the zone is towards north and along the Langar House Road which runs in the east-west direction and connects the zone to the Orr. Both these zones have a mix of apartments and villa projects along with plotted residential development.

PROPERTIES AVAILABLE IN THE CORRIDOR:

Gachibowli forms the core of the corridor. Gachibowli, followed by Manikonda has the highest share of supply. Together their share of supply is 69 %. The rate is highest in Gachibowli area and goes down by up to 20-25% as we move out to other peripheral localities of the corridor. About 40-50% of supply in the corridor is in the Rs. 50-90 lakh price bracket. While the Rs. 50-70 lakh bracket supply is distributed mainly across Manikonda, Gachibowli, Nallagandla and other localities, Gachibowli has almost 50-60% share of supply in the Rs. 70-90 lakh bracket. Higher the budget segment, higher the share of Gachibowli in supply. In the lower budget segment of Rs. 30-50 lakh, Manikonda hs most of the supply followed by Nallagandla. Most localties in the corridor offer maximum options in the Rs. 25-65 lakh price bracket.

The 3-BHK is the dominant format across almost all localities in the corridor. About 35% of these are available in the Rs. 45-65 lakh budget, Rs. 65 to Rs. 1 crore accounts for further 45 % share of the 3-BHK supply. Similarly, 55% of he 2-BHK options are available in the Rs. 45-65 lakh segment. About 40% of the 2-BHK options are in the Rs. 25-45 lakh price bracket. The corridor is witnessing considerable development activity and options are equally available in under-construction and ready-to-move-in projects.

BEST SECTORS TO INVEST IN A HOME

Based on rental demand in sectors:

Rental demand is overwhelmingly concentrated in Gachibowli and Manikonda because these are closest to IT/ITeS office space clusters. These office clusters are located not only in Gachibowli, but in the other localities towards east. The area also has well-developed support infrastructure. Rental demand in Nallagandla is more linked to its proximity to Serlingampally and Chandanagar areas. Other localities are situated at some distance from office space hubs and lack a demand driver which can create rental demand. Support infrastructure in these localities is also yet to evolve completely.

BASED ON HOME BUYING DEMAND IN SECTORS

Gachibowli and Manikonda have a major share (61%) of demand in the corridor. The reason for high demand is the same as that for rental demand – proximity to work place and presence of support infrastructure. Gachibowli has the highest share despite being the most expensive locality in the corridor. This shows that consumers put high emphasis on the habitability aspect. Demand for Appa Junction is a spill-over from localities towards the east Chevella Road. Other localities lack support infrastructure and are situated at some distance from office space hubs.

BEST BEDROOM CONFIGURATIONS TO BUY

Preferred buying and renting options:

Consumer prefers the 3-BHK format in the corridor. About 40% consumers are looking for the 3-BHK format in the Rs. 45-65 lakh bracket followed by 30% demand in the Rs. 65-85 lakh budget segment. The 2-BHK format is the second most preferred with bulk (55%) of the demand in the Rs. 45-65 lakh segment. The overlapping demand for 2 and 3-BHK units in the same budget segment is because consumers are willing to opt for smaller-sized apartments (2-BHK) at a higher price to stay in their preferred locality (Gachibowli).

PRICE CHANGES AND FUTURE PROSPECTS

Gachibowli corridor accounts for a bulk of residential development in Hyderabad. Consequently, it also has the highest supply and unsold inventory in the market. The market suffered from political instability, low sales volumes and large unsold stock. The political stability part has been addressed now. New project launches had come down as compared to earlier and hence, no more stock was added to the market. Sales have been steady for last few quarters and this has helped to clear the unsold stock.

Steady sales have kept the rates steady and, in some cases, the impact has been positive. The last 1-year price change shows similar positive impact on price levels.

PRICE MOVEMENT FOR TOP LOCALITIES BY CONSUER PREFERECE

The price movement in the top localities by consumer preference shows the slight shift in price level basis improved market conditions. While the percentage price change over the quarter is higher than average price change, the positive trend is in-line with market scenario over last one year. Gahibowli and Manikonda account for most of development activity as well as consumer demand within the corridor. And they offer mix of ready-to-move and under construction properties. Any positive change in the corridor will be reflected first in these markets. Except for Nallagandla, price hang in other localities is continuation of positive trend over last few quarters.

HYDERABAD

CORRIDOR NAMES

GACHIBOWLI: Narsinghi, Manikonda, Financial District, Gachibowli, Nallagandla, Tellapur, Kokapet, Appa Junction, Alkapur Township, Puppalaguda

---

MIYAPUR: Miyapur, Chandanagar, Nizampet an;d Bachupalli

GACHIBOWLI

GACHIBOWLI is the centre of development activity for both, commercial office space and residential segments. Presence of strong demand drivers in the IT/ITeS sector and continued improvement in infrastructure has attracted investors and end-users alike. The setting of new offices has led to new job opportunities and thus, boosted demand for residential real estate. In the future, depending on the purchasing power of employees, demand is expected to spread out. Residences at the periphery will continue to have demand from consumers. Employees of these IT/ITeS sector, who are in the lower-income brackets, will require affordable housing solutions. So, both, core and peripheral areas of this corridor will continue to see demand.

HIGHLIGHTS OF GACHIBOWLI CORRIDOR

- IT/ITES destination of Hyderabad
- Largest residential market
- Well established infrastructure
- Highest supply
- Good rental demand
- Better connectivity

DESTINATION : MIYAPUR

MIYAPUR: AN INVESTMENT HOTSPOT.

Miyapur and Chandanagar are the closest emerging residential, affordable locations from the IT hotspots of Hitec City and Gachibowli. The belt has transformed into a rapidly growing residential suburb. Proximity to IT corridors, improving infrastructure and affordability are making this area a preferred location for buyers.

INFRASTRUCTURE

Social infrastructure and connectivity jointly drive the real estate in an upcoming area. Located along the National Highway-9 (Pune-Hyderabad-Machilipatnam Highway), Miyapur enjoys seamless connectivity to the IT corridors of Hite City and Gachibowli. The upcoming 158 km, eight-lane, Outer Ring Road (ORR) connected with the Inner Ring Road and the upcoming Regional Ring Road will address the connectivity issues of the region.

The 12-km Miyapur to SR Nagar line could be the first metro rail stretch to the opened to the public later this year. Along with that, the work on the state-of-the-art Rs. 100-Crore Inter City bus Terminal (ICBT) on 500 acres at Miyapur is likely to begin soon. This will boost infrastructure in the area. Madhapr and Hitec City were the initial centers of development but they have been supplemented by Kukatpally, Miyapur, Bachupally and the surrounding localities.

Limited supply and high demand drove price appreciation of these locations. Some amount of price appreciation can also be accorded to the metro rail development along this corridor. Rental demand also remained strong as the rents appreciate by 5-10% year-on-year.

Here is an account how Miyapur has emerged as an upcoming residential corridor in the Hyderabad city.

> **CONSUMERS PREFER THE 2-BHK FORMAT IN THE CORRIDOR FROM BOTH HOUSE PURCHASE AND RENT PERSPECTIVE. IT HAS MORE THAN 50 % SHARE OF ONSUMER PREFERENCE.**
>
> **THE PRICE LEVEL IN SOME LOCALITIES HAS SEEN MARGINAL IMPROVEMENT, BUT THE OVER ALL PRICE LEVEL IS EXPECTED TO REMAIN FLAT.**

CURRENT STATUS OF THE CORRIDOR

The major infrastructure project in the corridor is the development of the Metro node at Miyapur. The Miyapur-LB Nagar Metro route is being developed as Corridor-1 with a distance of about 30 km. Miyapur to SR Nagar and SR Nagar to LB Nagar are referred to as Stage-2 and Srage-5, under the overall work plan of the Hyderabad Metro Rail network.

As per latest information, Phase-1 comprising Nagole to Mettuguda (State-1) and Miyapur-SR Nagar (Stage-2), will become operational in the first week of June 2016. Operationalization of this line will build connectivity to the corridor with other residential and commercial areas of Hyderabad. The State Government has announced plans for extending the Phase-1 of the Hyderabad Metro.

From the corridor's perspective, the Metro line is expected to be extended by a further13 km from Miyapur to BHEL and Patancheru. The timeline for implementation of this segment has not been declared. And Inter-City Bus Terminal (ICBT) is also planned to be developed at Miyapur. However, the development timeline for the same is not clear at present as the proposal is awaiting some clearances.

The corridor has faced water supply problem in the summer season, when due to low water level in the reservoirs, water supply was erratic coupled with low pressure I the government water supply network. Residents had to take recourse to purchasing water from private vendors. However, Hyderabad Metropolitan Water Supply and Sewerage

Board (HMWS&SB) is working on a plan to improve the pipeline work in Serilingampally Circle. This will improve the water supply of the corridor.

PRESENT RESIDENTIAL DEVELOPMENT

The corridor has a mix of apartments and plotted development. Bachupally has more plotted development options because of availability of land in the area. About 65 percent supply in the re-sale segment in the corridor is of multi-story apartments followed by builder floors/independent floors. The 2BHK format dominates across property types with a saleable area of 1000-1200 sq. ft. These accounts for 61 per cent supply in the re-sale segment with 3 BHK units are bigger in size with an average saleable area of 1500 sq. ft.

Miyapur, Chandanagar and Nizampet are among the top 10 localities by consumer preference in the city when it comes to purchase of a residential property. Similarly, in terms of consumers looking for rental options, Miyapur is again amongst the top 10 localities of Hyderabad. In terms of price level, the corridor caters to consumer preference in the lower price bracket.

More than 60 per cent of supply in the corridor in the resale segment is within the Rs. 20-40 lakh bracket. A further 29 per cent is in the Rs. 40-60 lakh segment. Together, the Rs. 20-60 lakh bracket accounts for 91 per cent supply in the resale segment. Evaluation of consumer preference in the corridor shows that almost the same percentage of consumers is looking for options within the Rs. 20-60 lakh segment. This highlights the price sensitive nature of demand in the market.

The average price level in the market is Rs. 3000 per sq. ft. Miyapur and Chandanagar have options in the Rs.3200-3400 per sq. ft price range, while capital values in Nizampet and Bachupally are on the lower side. The price level in these localities is in the Rs. 2400-2600 per sq. ft. range.

In line with general market trend, the price level in the corridor has been stagnant for some time. The overall price increment in all the localities of the corridor has been under 10 per cent for the last two years.

PROPERTIES AVAILABLE IN THE CORRIDOR

The corridor offers relatively less expensive options for consumers as compared to localities which are closer to IT/ITeS office hubs. Within the corridor, Miyapur and Chandanagar are established localities with higher capital values (Rs./sq. ft). Bachupally and Nizampet come next. This price differential impacts the budget and BHK format-wise spread of options.

More than 50 per cent supply is within Rs. 20-40 lakh bracket. A further 35 per cent is in the Rs. 40-60 lakh segment. Together, they account for 89 per cent supply. This highlights the price sensitive nature of the market. Most of the supply in the Rs. 20-40 lakh segment is in Nizampet and Miyapur localities. Miyapur, followed by Chandanagar and and Nizampet, accounts for bulk of supply in the Rs. 40-60 lakh bracket. In a price sensitive market, the smaller 2 BHK format with an average size of 1150 sq. ft dominates the supply; its small size helps a consumer to keep acquisition cost low. Most of the supply in the 2BHK format is in the Rs. 20-40 lakh price bracket wherein Nizampet leads with the highest share of 2 BHK options. The 3 BHK is the second most preferred category and most of it is concentrated in Miyapur. In budget terms, 60 per cent of 3 BHK options are in the Rs. 40-60 price bracket with almost 75 per cent being in the 1300-1700 sq. ft size range.

BEST SECTORS TO INVEST IN A HOME

Based on rental demand in sectors:

Rental demand in the corridor emanates from buyers looking fr residential options close to IT/ITeS office hubs in Madhapur and Gachibowli but cannot afford the options in localities which are close to them. Miyapur ranks high because of its location on National Highway-9 (NH-9) and presence of support infrastructure. It is easily accessible from different areas. Between Nizampet and Chandanagar, the former scores in terms of lower rentals while the latter is a well-established locality. Bachupally is still evolving and suffers from last mile connectivity and hence, the lower demand.

BASED ON HOME BUYING DEMAND IN SECTORS

Miyapur is the most preferred locality s it offers the best infrastructure as well as connectivity. It also has options across a wide price range from Rs. 20-40 lakh to Rs. 1-.1.2 crore. This gives flexibility to the consumers to choose as per their budget. Though, most consumers are looking for 3 BHK options in Miyapur. Most consumers in Chandanagar are looking for 2 BHK format in the Rs. 20-60 lakh price bracket. The demand for 3 BHK units is mainly in the Rs. 40-60 lakh budget. More than 60 percent demand in Nizampet is in the Rs. 20-40 lakh segment and for the 2 BHK format.

BEST BEDROOM CONFIGURATIONS TO BUY

Preferred buying and renting options.

Consumers prefer the 2 BHK format in the corridor from both house purchse as well as rent perspective. It has more than 50 per cent share of consumer preference as rent or purchase options. This can be explained by the fact that relatively smaller size of the 2 BHK apartments helps a buyer to keep the overall purchase cost on the lower side. About 84 per cent of consumer preference in the 2 BHK segment is in the Rs. 20-40 lakh segment followed by the Rs. 40-60 lakh bracket with only 16 per cent share. Almost 65 per cent of 2 BHK availability is in the 950-1200 sq. ft range and this give flexibility to consumers to choose and buy. In the Rs. 40-60 lakh bracket, 73 per cent demand is for 3 BHK segment while the rest is for 2 BHK formats.

PRICE CHANGES ANDFUTURE PROSPECTS 6 MONTHLY CHANGE: 1% YEARLY CHANGE: 4%

The price trend over last few quarters in the corridor reflects the overall slow market conditions. The price has been flat and has not seen any change over six months or one year Miyapur Corridor caters to a price sensitive demand segment which is looking for affordable homes. The purchasing ability of this segment is affected more by slow economic conditions. The sale had declined in the corridor leading to over-supply. But sale over last few quarters has been quite steady. And the price level in some localities has seen marginal improvement. But the overall price level is expected to remain flat or see marginal increase.

PRICE MOVEMENT FOR TOP LOCALITIES BY CONSUMER PREFERENCE

The price change in top localities by consumer demand over last quarter has varied across the localities. The price change varied from max of three per cent to minimum of 3 per cent. Miyapur, Gajularamaram and Pragathi Nagar continued the marginal price increment which they have witnessed over last few quarters. Price trend in Nizamapet has been positive for last few quarters. The present price drop could have happened by way of correction. The average price in previous quarter had reached a level which was highest over last few years and was not sustainable. Same is the case with Chandanagar.

Be it housing options, affordability or amenities Miyapur is one of the better choices for residential area.

Over view
Miyapur has a mix of residential, commercial and retail spaces. Miyapur has presence of companies from varied sectors such as IT, Pharmaceutical, apparel and industrial development. The second phase of metro will pass through Miyapur and is expected to boost reality.
Resident's review
Miyapur is well-connected via roads and public transport system. It is close to schools, colleges, hospitals, banks and markets. It is also close to companies like Miscrosoft, Wipro, TCS, Infosys, Capgemini, CMC, CTS, Infotech, etc.

Miyapur is easily accessible from Miyapur Main Road and near metro station, bus stops, Cinema Halls, food joints, hospitals, schools and colleges. It is just 5 km from Histec City, 7 km from Gachibowli and 5 km from JNTU.

Miyapur is a very promising suburb with excellent connectivity to IT Centers like Histec Csity, education centre of JNTU and Pharma centre of Bachupally. It has very good road access as well as new metro which are coming up and most promising destination for the next 5 years.

MIYAPUR

Affordable houses being offered is a big positive for the corridor. Many offices belonging to the IT/ITes sector located nearby employ high salaried professionals as well. Most of the employee based of these IT/ITeS companies is young and in the lower income level (relative to industry salary levels). Such employees seek affordable rentals and purchase options. The Miyapur Corridor with its competitive price level, is perfectly placed to address this demand. However, the price level is not expected to see major gains as this would put the market out of reach for people who form the consumer base for the corridor. Overall, the corridor offers good residential options to consumers looking for affordable homes in a well-established area with good connectivity and social infrastructure.

HIGHLIGHTS OF MIYAPUR CORRIDOR

Price sensitive market
Affordable housing available
Metro connectivity
Good social infrastructure
Better road connectivity
Stagnant price

MIYAPUR RANKS HIGH ON AFFORDABILITY

Many people feel this could be the best time to invest in Hyderabad. People are rigt. The city has fared better than most other active real estate markets in the country. This calls for attention because post a prolonged state of lull and limited conversions, the investment climate is ridden with a positive streak.

The real estate market seems right. Project deliveries have picked momentum and we have been conversing with some agents and they sound positive about the developers.

Miyapur is one of the top localities in the real estate forum where enquiries usually pour in. It has been identified as one of the growth corridors in the Corridors of Growth report by Magic bricks. Few key points about the locality are given below.

RESIDENTIAL SUPPLY IN MIYAPUR

Of all the listed properties, over 60 per cent is in the resale segment with a price tag 0f 20-40 lakh. Prospective buyers have been enquiring about projects within this range as well. Close to 65 per cent user enquiries have been recorded within this segment.

Hyderabad being mostly a price sensitive market, this area has come up to suit the needs of consumers. In this regard, supply is in sync with demand. The good part is that a large portion f the residential supply is in the ready-to-move-in category.

CURRENT PROPERRTY PRICES

The larger view of the market suggests that 1 BHK units are mostly in the range of Rs. 12-31 lakh with sizes of 480-975 sq.ft. The price range of 2 BHK units is Rs. 15-52 lakh and mostly within 1600 sq.ft. If you are in for a bigger investment, the 3 BHK units herein are in the size range of 1200-2500 sq,ft, These cost anywhere up to Rs. 90 lakh depending upon the kind of amenities.

EXISTING INFRASTRUCTURE

Metro has been a game changer and the government is proposing to extend the reach of Corridor 1 whihv terminates at Miypur at present. If it takes off, Miyapur will boast of significant improvement in connectivity to the west and north-west. At present, Chandanagar, Miyapur and Nizampet have good connectivity and accessibility to other parts of the city through road and existing suburban railway network. This will improve further when the Hyderabad Metro becomes operational. Reportedly, the trial runs between Miyapur and Sanjeeva Reddy Naga have been going onsmoothly.

Call it a price advantage, Hydeabad has always championed when it comes to affordable properties. Approximately, 55 per cent of the total supply is in th affordable segment – below Rs. 4,000 per sq. ft. for a prospective buyer, this gives a lot of choices. Among the popular localities within this price are Sainikpuri, Kukatpally, Manikonda, Miyapur and Chananagar.

Travelling 22.5 kilometres northwest of Hyderabad will take you to Miyapur which is one of the growing residential areas with high rise residential apartments, communities and other social infrastructures. Miyapur which is a part of Greater Hyderabad and administered by GHMC and developed by HMDA is an extension of Kukatpally and Nizampet area, and is developing into a major residential, educational and commercial hub. It is one of Hyderabad's busiest places at the head of the Miyapur – L.B Nagar high-density traffic corridor. Miyapur landmarks various commercial establishments and is inclusive of a number of water bodies such as Miyapur cheruvu, Ameenpur Lake, Hafeezpur, Gangaram, Miyapur patel and Madeeguda Lakes.

The commercial and residential projects are on the rise due to its proximity to IT and Industrial hubs. It is designated as a "high-rise" zone and the demand for real-estate has skyrocketed. The area is about 10 km from Hitec City, 18 km from Punjagutta and 21 km from Secunderabad and is strategically situated on National Highway 9 with IT, pharmaceutical and industrial development areas. Miyapur houses various government establishments such as Telangana State Disaster Response and Fire Services, Cyber Crime Police Station, TSSPDCL, Hyderabad Metropolitan Water Supply and Sewerage Board, BSNL, TSRTC, eSeva, NHAI, TSPCB and many more.

The social infrastructure of the area is also well developed. The area has a number of good hospitals such as Pranam, Srikara, Maxcure and many more which provide 24/7 medical emergency and ambulance services. Miyapur is well connected via roads and public transport system. It is close to schools, colleges, hospitals, banks and markets. It is close to companies like Microsoft, Wipro, Infosys, TCS, Capgemini, CMC, CTS, Infotech and many more. There are a number of governament and private educational institutions in Miyapur such as state government schools, Central and International schools. The proximity to IT hubs, good schools and hospitals has made Miyapur, a favourite destination for families.

The capital and the rental values in Miyapur are still low compared to other developed areas of the city, making it among the affordable places. There are bunch

of grocery shops nearby. So, even if one run out of things, one can fetch it within no time. Miyapur is well connected by road, rail and air and is becoming a hub for travelers within Hyderabad city. Share autos, cabs, rental cars and buses are widely available. Hafeezpet is the nearest MMTS station for Miyapur. Rajiv Gandhi airport is 40 kms away, Secunderabad airport is around 22 kms away and Begumpet airport is 15 km south west of Miyapur.

Apart from the high-rise buildings, the area also has some proper residential colonies maintained by welfare associations. The capital and the rental values in Miyapur are affordable as compared to other areas of the city.

Miyapur also has multiplexes and single screen theatres, good restaurants, shopping places, and some open spaces to enjoy nature. With all these in place, Miyapur's fast paced development is attracting investors.

DESTINATION BALANAGAR

Balanagar is one of the major industrial areas in North West Hyderabad. Hospitals, Super Markets, Banks, ATMs, Medical Shops, Function Halls, Petrol Pumps, Eateries, etc exist within 3 km radius.

Infused with Government and private industries, Balanagar is expanding as a residential area over the years.

With increasing number of government and private industries infused into the area, Balanagar is growing as a preferred residential area over the years.

Located in the north western belt of Hyderabad, Balanagar is one of the preferred residential localities in Hyderabad which is about 13 km from Hitec city and 6 km from Begumpet. Balanagar is an industrial area that houses many central government funded heavy industrial units such as IDPL, HAL and private companies like Khaitan fans, Usha fans, Apar from these big companies, Balanagar is home to many small and medium businesses.

A considerable chunk of people are employed at various offices and manufacturing units in this area and it is gaining importance as a residential area due to its connectivity and pricing. The spillover due to saturation of Gachibowli, Kondapur, Kukatpally and the surrounding areas has made it a preferred location of services class employees.

INVESTMENT IN BALANAGAR

Balanagar is home to many service class employees and is improving as a residential area for investment.

Located in the north western belt of Hydrabad, Balanagar is a strategically placed locality in the city. It is best known for housing several central governments funded heavy industrial units and private companies. Not only this, it is also home for various small and medium sized businesses. Balanagar is home to service class employees and is witnessing considerable importance in terms of residential area for investment. Let us know what makes Balanagar a preferred destination to invest?

CONNECTIVITY AND PREFERENCE

It is located on the National Highway 7 between Hyderabad and Kurnool.

The locality is about 13 km from Hitec City and 6 km from Begumpet and in close proximity to other developed localities.

As Gachibowli, Kondapur, Kukatpally and surrounding areas have already reached a saturation point in terms of infrastructure development and availability of homes. Therefore, Balanagar has become a preferred location of service class employees.

The locality is well-connected to other areas via autos, RTC buses and shared autos.

PRICING

What kind of residences can you find? Balanagar has the potential to offer varied residential housing types such as flats, residential plots, houses and villas. Potential property buyers with limited budget and working in proximity to Balanagar can consider it for its varied housing types priced affordably. Professionals working in nearby Begumpet and Panjagutta commercial establishments can also find a home in Balanagar in their budget.

Connectivity is one of the main factors which has to be considered while setting up an office for business and Balanagar matches the criterion. In fact the area is developing so fast that now it's very difficult to get a plot in this area. The colonies and residential segments developing here are of high class.

Here are many autos, shared autos plying in the area. Also, Balanagar has a good connectivity with other areas through RTC buses. Even if one doesn't own a vehicle, either two-wheeler or four-wheeler, there are a plethora of options available for commuting. With so many options available conveyance as such is not a problem.

Jubilee Bus Stand in Secunderabad is 10 km from Balanagar while the Secunderabad Railway station is 8 km. Mahatma Gandhi Bus Stand is at a distance of 15 km while the Rajiv Galndhi International Airport is 38 km away. The area is about 30 minutes' drive to Hitech city and about an hour drive to Gachibowli.

The Jeedimetla Rod and the Mumbai Highway connect localities, Bharat Nagar Station is roughly 15 kms from Jeedimetla Road and is the nearest station.

The social infrastructure in Balanagar is well established. The area has many multi-functional spaces that offer an overall shopping and entertainment experience.

There are many shopping centers in the vicinity of the area. Begumpet and Panjagutta area also offer a variety of shopping options. For daily needs there are many grocery stores in the area itself. In few colonies the vegetable vendors put up stalls and sell fresh fruits and vegetables.

The area has many restaurants and food joints which cater to the need of the residents. Schools, colleges and hospitals too are present in the vicinity. If one wishes to travel a little further from Panjagutta, then one will have lot of shopping options in Ameerpet and at a reasonable cost.

Affordability is an important factor in residential development. Balanagar is considered to be one of the most affordable localities in the city. Probably this is the reason why it has emerged as a major residential hub for government employees, industrialists, service class employees, and businessmen. There are apartments, independent houses and few open plots available. It costs around Rs. 15 lakh for 1BHK flat. For a 2BHK and 3 BHK of 700 sq.ft. 1235 sq.ft and 1344 sq.t-1949 sq,ft, the cost comes around 18 lakh-42 lakh and Rs. 37 lakh-Rs. 87 lakh respectively. For a 1 BHK apartment, the rental value is around Rs. 6000. For 2 BHK and 3 BHK, it ranges between Rs. 7,000 to Rs. 12000 and Rs. 10,000 to Rs. 18,000 respectiely.

When limited budget and proximity to the workplace are the main criteria, then Balanagar offers affordable housing options for those employed in any of the industrial units is the area. Those who are employed on a modest monthly income in Begumpet and Panjagutta can find a house in Balanagar that will suit their budget.

- Balanagar is a well-developed and witnessing infrastructure development.
- The Hyderabad Metropolitan Development Authority (HMDA) has sanctioned the construction of a new flyover between Balanagar Crossroads and Narsapur Crossroads.
- Many internal roads within the localities are under repair and re-development.
- It is also home various small and medium sized businesses. Balangar is home to service class employees.
- It is witnessing considerable residential investment.
- It is located on the National Highway 7 between Hyderabad and Kurnool.
- The locality is about 13 km from Hitec City and 6 km from Begumpet and in close proximity to other developed localities.
- Potential property buyers with limited budget and working in proximity to Balanagar can consider it for its varied housing types priced affordably.

RESIDENTS VIEW

- Balanagar is a industrial area developed by APIIC, surrounded by semi-residential area, occupied by business and working class people. It is 6 km from Panjagutta or paradise circle connected with public transport and MMTS train.
- Balanagar is one of the major industrial estates in India located in North West side of Hyderabad. Several governments owned industries are established in this location. IDPL,

IDL, NRSA, HAL, BHEL R&D are few amongst them. USHA Fans Company and Kediaya, Khaithan fan companies are located in this place.

- It is a friendly neighbourhood. Facilities like hospitals, Supermarkets, banks, ATMs, medical shops, function halls, lodges, restaurants, etc are within 3 km radius. Major shopping/commercial places are within 8 k radius.

BALANAGAR is located in the north western belt of **Hyderabad**. It is about 13km from Hitec city and 6 km from **Begumpet**. **Balanagar** is an industrial area that houses many central governments funded heavy industrial units such as **IDPL, HAL** and private companies like **Kaitan fans, Usha fans**. Apart from these big companies, **Balanagar** is home to many small and medium businesses. A considerable chunk of people are employed at various offices and manufacturing units in this area. It is gaining importance as a residential area due to its connectivity and pricing.

The spillover due to saturation of **Gachibowli, Kondapur, Kukatpally** and surrounding areas has made it a preferred location of service class employees. In fact the area is developing so fast that now it's very difficult to get a plot in this area. The colonies and residential segments developing here are of high class.

Balanagar is well connected to other areas of the city. There are many auto, shared autos plying in the area. Also, **Balanagar** has a good connectivity with other areas through RTC buses. Also, **Balanagar** has a good connectivity with other areas through RTC buses. Even if one doesn't own a vehicle, either two wheeler or four wheeler, there are a plethora of options available for commuting. With so many options available conveyance as such is not a problem. **Jubilee Bus Stand** in **Secunderabad** is 10 km from **Balanagar** while the **Secunderabad** Railway station is 8 km**. Mahatma Gandhi Bus Stand** is at a distance of 15km while **Rajiv Gandhi International Airport** is 38 km away. The area is about 30 minutes' drive to **Hitec city** and about an hour drive to **Gachibowli.** The **Jeedimetla** Road and the **Mumbai Highway** connect localities. **Bharat Nagar Station** is roughly 15 kms from **Jeedimetla** Road and is the nearest station.

The social infrastructure in **Balanagar** is well established. The area has many multi-functional spaces that offer an overall shopping and entertainment experience. There are many shopping centers in the vicinity of the area. **Begumpet** and **Panjagutta** areas also offer a variety of shopping options. For daily needs there are many grocery stores in the area itself. In few colonies the vegetable vendors put up stalls and sell free fruits and vegetables. The area has many restaurants and food joints which cater to the need of the residents. Schools, colleges and hospitals too are present in the vicinity. If one wishes to travel a little further from **Panjagutta**, then one will have lot of shopping options in **Ameerpet** and at a reasonable cost.

Affordability is an important factor in residential development. **Balanagar** is considered to be one of the most affordable localities in the city. Probably this is the reason why it has emerged as a major residential hub for government employees, industrialists, service class employees, and businessmen. There are apartments, independent houses and few open plots available. The locality witnessed maximum availability of 3 and 4 BHK flats. When limited budget and proximity to workplace are the main criteria, then **Balanagar** offers affordable housing options for those employed at any of the industrial units in the area. Those who are employed on a modest monthly income in commercial establishments that are located in **Begumpet** and **Panjagutta** can find a house in **Balanagar** that will suit their budget.

BALANAGAR AREA KEY TAKEAWAYS

- Balanagar in North-West Hyderabad is a part of the popular industrial and manufacturing belt developed by the Andhra Pradesh Industrial Infrastructure Corporation Ltd Housing.
- Several government owned industries such as IDPL, IDL, NRSA, HAL, Bharat Heavy Electronics Limited R&D, others namely USHA Fans and Kediaya, Khaithan Fan companies are located here
- The area is about 30 minutes' drive to Hitec City (14 km) and about an hur drive to Gachibowli (20 km).
- Affordable housing attracts buyers.
- The Jeedimetla Road and the Mumbai Highway connects localities. Bharat Nagar Station is roughly 15 kms from Jeedimetla Road and is the nearest station.
- The area is majorly driven by investors. Interested end-users are belonging to the working class.

DESTINATION NALLAGANDLA

- **NALLAGANDLA** is a fast-developing locality with proximity to all established localities.
- The area is well-connected to the IT hub through the Outer Ring Road (ORR).
- The Nehru Outer Ring Road and NH 65, both are situated within 6 km radius.
- Over 10 new residential projects are launched with possession date by end 2018.

RESIDENT'S REVIEW:

NALLAGANDLA is a very good location. It is near Citizen Hospital, 2 km to Lingampally MMTS Station, 3 km to BHEL Circle, 7.5 km to Wipro Junction (Wipro, Microsoft, Polaris, Infosys,) 9 km to Kondapur (Kothaguda Junction).

NALLAGANDLA is one of the fastest developing localities in Hyderabad. It is a very good location with most of the things very nearby. It is a very peaceful with less traffic but secured. It is very close to Lingampally Station, BHEL, Gachibowli IT, ORR and Chanda Nagar. It has excellent schools, markets and public transport.

NALLAGANDLA is a very peaceful and serene locality. It is an upcoming area with proximity to multinational IT companies and IT parks. Schools, banks, ATMs and hospitals are available nearby the locality.

NALLAGANDLA PREFERRED INVESTMENT DESTINATION

Nallagandla has proven to be a very consistent investment opportunity with rents being among the highest in the city.

Nallagandla is known in Hyderabad as one of the most strategically placed areas i., between Information Technology (IT) hub and BHEL. What really makes the area as a preferred residential hub is its proximity to the Lingampally MTS (Multi Modal Transport System) Station which is hardly at a 1 km distance. Whether you are an investor, buyer or a migrating It professional, it might seem fruitful to invest in Nallagandla.

Why you should consider Nallagandla as an investment destination?

- ✓ Nallagandla is situated between the Outer Ring Road (ORR) and the Old Mumbai Road which further makes it accessible to all major parts of the city such as BHEL, Hitech City, Banjara Hills and Gachibowli.

- ✓ The locality is just 4 km away from the Lingampally railway station and at 8 km distance from Wipro Junction and 3 km from the University of Hyderabad.

- ✓ Nallaganla is well connected with other parts of Hyderabad via Tellapur road, MG road, Gachibowli road and Old Mumbai highway.

- ✓ National Highway 65 is 3 km away from the locality which ensures its swift connectivity with other localities and states too.

INFRASTRUCTURE DEVELOPMENTS IN PIPELINE

- ✓ Very soon the locality will get a flyover which is going to address the problem of traffic on the old highway to Mumbai. The flyover is spread over a length of 21 meters with a 7.50 meter carriageway.

- ✓ Also the locality is witnessing a lot of repair development in terms of filling of potholes and maintenance of roads.

AMENITIES SUITING YOUR LIFESTYLE

Whether you buy an apartment, lot or a villa in Nallagandla, the locality offers varied types of amenities suiting your lifestyle. Some of the amenities offered under the residential housing projects in the area are-

- Club house
- Jogging & strolling track
- Power back up
- Car parking
- Lift
- Swimming pool

- Outdoor tennis court
- Water storage
- Round the clock security
- Pied Gas Connection
- Electrical chimney and RO water filter pre-fitted in kitchen
- Dance studio
- Gated colony – plots.

Before making your selection always ensure to assess your requirements in terms of property size, location, infrastructure and proximity to schools, hospitals and other day to day convenience stores. So, if you are planning to invest in Nallagandla then you must not wait as the area has all the potentials to give higher returns in future.

Apart from its potential of offering good rental returns, Nallagandla is strategically located with upcoming physical and social infrastructure.

NALLAGANDLA, an area sandwiched between Gachibowli and BHEL zoomed onto prominence on the real estate radar with the development of IT and ITeS sector. It is a relatively new residential option that is fast finding a foothold in the real estate market of Hyderabad. The locality is transforming into a full-fledged residential hub due to its developing infrastructure and improved connectivity. "Nearly 60-70 percent of the housing demand comes from people working in he IT companies while BHEL also contributes to about 30 per cent of the housing demand.

The locality is hardly one km from the Lingampally MMTS station. It is also placed between the Outer Ring Road (ORR) and the Old Mumbai Road. As a result, swift connectivity and easy accessibility with all important junctions, Hitec City, Banjara Hills and other parts of the city is a clear advantage. The Rajiv Gandhi International Airport at Shamshabad is 39 km from here and is easily accessible via the ORR. Lingampally Railway Station is the nearest station to the area located at over 2-km distance.

The area shares its neighbourhood with Nizampet, Miyapur, Beeramguda, Gachibowli and Kukatpally. In fact, Nallagandla Lake is another attraction which adds value to the location. Nallagandla is still developing and has ample green area. The locality is livable as all basic amenities such as grocery shops, ATMs, schools and colleges are available within close distance. The social infrastructure in the area is also pretty good. Nallagandla houses a number of good schools, colleges, healthcare centers, banks and supermarkets.

Apart from its potential of offering good ental returns, the locality is strategically locaged with upcoming physical and social infrastructure. The properties available in this locality definitely feature amongst the top five investment destinations as of now. The average rate is INR 4,500.00 per sq. ft. Interestingly, apartments in Nallagandla hold high rental values. Majority of buyers in the area are IT professionals and the government officials working in BHEL are also raising demand. The rental value of 3 BHK units is between INR 20,000-35,000 per month and for 2 BHK units it is between INR 10,000-20,000 per month. Since the area is undergoing a transformation, the time could be right to make an investment. The housing inventory consists of villas, builder floors, plots and apartments. You can buy a 2 BHK apartment in the price bracket of INR 28.00 lakhs to INR 65.00 lakhs with sizes varying from 875 to 1668 sq. ft. Further, the price range for a 3 BHK apartment is INR 50.00 lakh to over 1.20 crore, sizes varying from 1250-1300 sq.ft.

As an investor if you are looking to buy a spacious apartment to further reap profitable returns in Hyderabad, Nallagandla van be a good choice. Due to an increase in the prominence quotient, it might be safe to mention that Nallagandla's potential of return on investment is high as Hyderabad is a growing market.

DESTINATION NARSINGI

NARSINGI LOCALITIES

The inventories in the locality are apartments, villas, residential plots and residential houses. **Narsingi** mostly offers housing to mid segment and upper segment buyers. The most demanded inventories are 3 BHK followed by 2 BHK apartments. Most supplied budget range is the Rs. 40-60 lakh segment.

Narsingi is located strategically in **Hyderabad** wherein the area is intersected by NH 44. It is surrounded by various areas such as **Narsampalle, Kaslapur, Seripalle, shailpet**, among others. Some of the important roads intersecting the locality are **Toopran-Mirzapalli road**, **Cheruvu road**, etc. Mirzapalli railway station is the nearest station to the locality.

There are 2 and 3 BHK residential houses available within a budget range of 65 lakh - 1 crore. Units of 2 BHK and 3 BHK are sized 750-1270 sq. ft and 1235-2540 sq.ft respectively. 4 BHK and 5 BHK units ar available between 94 lakh – 12 crore and 65 – 70 lakh respectively. For villas, it can be anywhere between 2-4 crore depending upon the amenities.

KEY TAKEAWAYS AT NARSINGI

- **Narsingi** is an established area in the Ranga Reddy district of Hyderabad, situated around 8-km from **Gachibowli** via the **Nanakramguda** Road.
- It is located adjacent to the Outer Ring Road which makes it better in terms of connectivity.
- The neighbouring areas include **Manikonda Gachibowli, Gandipet and Nanakramguda**.
- I you intend to buy a luxury home in Hyderabad, **Narsingi** can definitely be a part of the list as it offers a number of such homes.
- The nearest MMTS situated is at Hitec City via the **Narsingi-Nanakramguda** Service Road.
- Large acres of plots are available in the locality that helps to keep up the water level, so there is sufficient supply of water.
- There are a lot of gated communities and societies in the locality making it safe and secure.
- **Narsingi** can b a good option for housing for the working IT professionals of nearby places like **Gachibowli** and **Manikonda.**
- Since the area is still developing, there is limited service of buses in the locality. One needs personal transportation to commute.
- Most available property type in the locality is apartments and residential plots. These inventories have all basic amenities such as parks, swimming pool, club, car parking, among other.

Narsingi is a prime location in Hyderabad. All facilities like malls, schools, markets, hospitals, banks and ATMS are available in this locality. There is scope for further development here. It is adjacent to ORR and 10-km to **Gahibowli,** 11=km to **Mehadipatnam** and 20-km to the **Airport.**

NARSINGI offers many gated community villas and apartments at affordable prices making it a good residential area.

Travelling 10 m from the **Jawharlal Nehu Outer Ring Road** flyover takes you to the beautiful residential area called **Narsingi.** The area which was regarded a small village famous for livestock and a decade ago has undergone a drastic change. It now has well cemented roads, an underground drainage system, water supply connections, connectivity, banks, schools, etc. This de elopement has made the value for land shoot up. The area is also witnessing some high rise construction work. Recent developments around the area have boosted property values and is attracting professionals. High rise apartments, gated community villas and open plots are available in the area. Majority of the crowd residing here is employed in the IT and ITeS sectors.

ORR's major junction in **Narsingi** enhances its connectivity. Additionally, the presence of 60 feet road too works in the area's favour, **TSRTC** buses have regular halts at **Narsingi Bus Stop**, thereby connecting the area to other parts of the city. Autos and shared autos too are available for short distance commutation. As mentioned earlier, **Narsingi** is home to many professionals working in the IT and ITeS sectors. **Narsingi** is located strategically in Hyderabad wherein the area is intersected by NH 44. It is surrounded by various areas such as **Narsampalle, Kaslapur, Seripalle, shailpet,** among others. Some of the important road intersecting the locality is **Toopran** – **Mirzapalli** road, **Cheruvu** road, etc. **Mirzapalli railway station is** the nearest station to the locality. Buses **from here connect to Mehdipatnam, Tolichowki and Secunderabad.** The area is best suited for working professionals. It is well connected with rest of the city and its proximity to social infrastructure makes it a good area to live in. I share a 2 BHK apartment with my friend and the rental is also affordable. Above all, the place is calm and peaceful.

The social infrastructure is also pretty good in the area with a number of good schools, colleges, hospitals, restaurants, banks, super market, petrol pump and pharmacy. **Narsingi** is home to a major hospital coupled with few smaller nursing homes. The area has many daily needs stores thereby residents here need not travel far for small grocery requirements. It is a good area for bachelors and families as well. It is slowly developing into a full-fledged residential area.

Real estate prices in **Narsingi** could be termed as fairly affordable. There are some projects in the area boasting of more advanced facilities and are priced even higher. While there are apartments in 2 BHK forma, many projects have 3 BHK format apartments presumably due to comparatively lower real estate prices. For a 2 BHK unit of 750-1270 sq feet, the cost is between INR 27-63 lakh. For a 3 BHK flats of 1235-2540 sq. ft, the cost comes between INR 41-96 lakh. For villas, the price is higher. For a 3 BHK and 4 BHK villas of 3135-4024 and 2600-6150 sq.ft, the price comes between INR 2-4 crore. For residential plots and commercial land, the price range is INR 60 lakh – INR 1.5 crore and 2-4 crore respectively. For a 2 BHK apartment, the rental ranges from INR 8400-14,000. For a 3 BHK and 4 BHK, the rental starts from INR 15,000. Compared to other residential hubs, **Narsingi** is affordably priced.

=======

DESTINATION KONDAPUR

The advantages of amenities make Kondapur one of the best residential localities in the city.

OVER VIEW

- Kondapur is a central locality in Hyderabad with proximity to areas such as Hafeezpet, Nallagandla, Chanda Nagar, Miyapur, amongst others.
- Kondapur has developed into a modern business hub as it is close to business districts of Higtec City and Gacchibowli.

RESIDENT'S REVIEW

- Kondapur is a peaceful residential locality with parks, schools, restaurants, hospitals. This locality is very close to Hitec City and Financial District. This locality is also close to super markets and banks.
- Kondapur is a great locality to settle in, with schools, hospitals, malls, restaurants in the vicinity. It gives opportunity for a balanced work life. Ity has got good public transport and communication facilities.
- Kondapur is a very nice location. It is near to schools, hospitals, markets, shopping malls. It is well-connected to Gacchibowli, Hitec City, Hafizpet, Chanda Nagar and Lingampally.

Kondapur, with its growing number of IT companies is becoming a pivotal area for startup business and working-class population. The area is a suburb which is in close proximity to Gacchibowli and Hitec City and is one of the most sought-after locality for residential and commercial establishments. This in turn has increased the real estate value of the area, marking a rise in reality demand. Kondapur, which is located in the Cyberabad information technology zone, in the Ranga Reddy district of Hyderabad Metropolitan Region is close to the Madhapur-Kondapur stretch. It is around 14 kms from Banjara Hills and around 23 kms from Secunderabad. Its close proximity to Old Mumbai Road, Gachibowli-Miyapur Road, and Hitech City Road makes it an easy residential road also serves as an excellent route for transportation. The public transport system here is good. So, easy commutation is an advantage for this place.

We have TSRTC buses connecting almost all areas. Buses are available frequently to areas such as Koti, Secunderabad, Patancheru, Dilsukhnagar. The International Airport is at a distance of approximately 30 kms from here and the nearest railway station is located at Hafizpet, which is around 4 km from Kondapur. The metro line will also be available soon from Hitech City stop. Apart from these, the locals also frequently use auto-rickshaws.

The social and civic infrastructure is quite good in Kondapur, reaching out to an array of schools, institutions, hospitals, supermarkets, theatres, and exhibition centers. Almost every amenity is available here in Kondapur. Be it banking, Super markets, theatres, Kondapur houses them all. The area also provides a wide choice of restaurants and street food. Cultural center of Shilparamam is 2 km away and the botanical garden is also nearby for spending leisure time. Unlike other suburbs, Kondapur enjoys green environment because of the Botanical Garden and is a green feast to behold in the concrete jungle.

There is a steep rise in the residential demand accounting to a surge of employees migrating to Kondapur. Kondapur presently is crowded with multi-storey apartments of both semi-luxury and luxury caliber. The booming IT sector is redefining the real estate market of Kondapur. Along with it, the addition of metro line has also triggered the real estate flux of Kondapur.

Kondapur can be a good residential choice, if you are looking for a developed, well-connected residential area.

==========

DESTINATION L.B NAGAR

L.B. NAGAR provides a comfortable living with its proximity, connectivity and affordability.

RESIDENT'S REVIEW:

L.B. Nagar has good connectivity, and at a walkable distance. This is a locality for everyone, safe for kids, lot of space for kids to play, lot of greenery around. It is a no pollution zone.

It is near proposed corporate, global hospital. Metro station is within 1 km. The travel time to Nalgonda x roads is 15 minutes, Koti is 20 minutes away, Nadargul IT park is 10 minutes away and Shamshabad airport is 35 minutes away.

LB Nagar is near Kotta Peta Fruit market. Hospitals, vegetable market and Registrar office is within proximity. It is a good neighbourhood and has good theatres. Bus station is also present. There are some good schools too.

LB Nagar is known as a residential and commercial hub housing some of the major commercial centers.

At present, metro work between Miyapur to LB Nagar line (Red Line) is under works. The distance covers almost 25 areas.

L B NAGAR or Lal Bahadur Nagar is one among the many major commercial and residential centers of Hyderabad. One of the fastest growing suburbs of the city LB Nagar provides many affordable housing options. The area is near to Kothapet, Nagole, Vanasthalipuram, NTR Nagar and Saroornagar. The area has fully grown in terms of development and connectivity. The proximity to outer ring road (ORR) and high frequency of buses on this route has given some extra mileage to this area.

This area provides a comfortable living and has all the required amenities. The area suits best for the middle income group as it provides a variety of residential options in a decent budget. People chose this area because it offers the most affordable housing options. The area has all provisions to live a comfortable life. The proximity and connectivity are an added advantage for the area.

There are number of buses of TSRTC frequently having service in B. Nagar, linking it with the city and surrounding suburbs. It is also a major stop and pick up point for long distance buses to Vijayawada, Rajahmundry, Chennai, Guntur, Nellore, Visakhapatnam, Nalgonda, Miyaluda, Khammam and Suryapet. Dilsukhnagar, which is very close to LB Naga, has the biggest bus depot of the city. Malakpet is the nearest MMTS station from LB Nagar The area also has smooth connectivity to ORR and inner ring road. LB Nagar provides a great transit facility to any art of the city.

The social and civic infrastructure in the area is good. There are a number of good hospitals and medical services in this area. The quality of schools and colleges is also good, with some of international standards. LB Nagar also has plenty of super markets and kirana shops. NTR Nagar Ryathu Bazar is just 1.5 km from this place and there are many supermarkets within a radius of 2-3 kms. The good point is, even after so much commercialization the area scores high on greenery. The area has colony culture so the colonies maintain greenery within the premises. The area is self-contained as I have many supermarkets and retail outlets. The schools, colleges and hospitals in this area are also in plenty. The area has everything for a comfortable living. It has grocery stores, corporate stores, schools, parks, hospitals and banks within a radius of 5 kms.

LB Nagar provides affordable housing as well. For 1 BHK and 2 BHK apartments, the prices are within the range of any middle and upper-middle-class people's earnings.

========

DESTINATION KOMPALLY

Kompally is a good residential area with a peaceful and pollution free environment.

- Kompally is a growing hub for warehouse and cargo-oriented business.
- The area is accessible via NH 7, Doolapally Road and Bolarum-Kompally Road.
- It is rated as 4.5 on the basis of great environment, commuting facilities and facilities nearby Magic bricks readers.
- Kompally is a calm residential locality with easy access from Secunderabad Railway Station and Hyderabad International Airport. The roads are good with no major bottlenecks. It is situated close to schools, colleges, movie halls, etc.
- Kompally is a very great location. It is ear main road an at walkable distance from the main road, public transport depot. It is near premium restaurants, parks, sports club, health care, schools. It is well connected to railway station.
- Kompally is just 6 lanes, NH 7 towards Nagpur. It is just 10 kms from Paradise, Secunderabad. The Outer Ring Road is connected at Kandlakoya, which is 3 km from Kompally. The famous Basar – Saraswathi Temple is a four-and-a-half-hour drive from here.

KOMPALLY IS A GOOD PLACE TO RESIDE

The locality has easy accessibility to Gachibowli, Hitec City, Kukatpally, Whitefield and other nearby areas through the Outer Ring Road (ORR).

Kompally is an upcoming suburb of Hyderabad which is emerging as a residential area. It is about 24 km from Hitec City, 15 km from Secunderabad and 18 km from Punjagutta. The area offers a serene living atmosphere which is fast attracting investors. The area is well connected and has many reputed school and colleges. The area which used to be a small village with a good green cover is slowly transforming itself into a center of buzzing activities. The residential sector mainly consists of gated communities. As the area is still developing, a gated community is a good option as it is equipped with all facilities. The area has good roads, in house service men and excellent security. The civic infrastructure of the area is well in place and social infrastructure is good. The area has some good schools, hospitals and market places. All daily needs are available in close vicinity. The green cover and quality of people living here make this area very cordial and relaxed. The residents of the area don't mind travelling as it extra everyday as it well maintained gives them access to great amenities. This area has housing for high and mid segment buyers and investors. It is also seeing growth in terms of commercial outlets. It has potential and is witnessing a steady growth.

KOMPALLY IS A CLEAR CHOICE FOR A FAMILY LOOKING FOR AN AFORDABLE BUT SERENE AREA TO LIVE IN.

Kompally is only one hour's drive away from Hyderabad and offers apartments in the budget range of Rs. 30-40 lakh.

AFFORDABLE LOCALITY

Property prices in Kompally are in the lower price range. From Rs. 3,173 per sq ft in January-March 2016, property prices in Kompally in October stand as Rs. 2,675 sq.ft. This amounts to about 15 per cent decline in the property prices. This may sound tempting to end-users who have been mulling to buy a house near Hyderabad. If you have already selected a property then chances are that its price tag has moved towards the lower side.

WHAT CAN YOU FIND HERE?

One can get flats and plots in the area. A 1BHK flat in the size of 340-540 sq. ft costs anywhere between Rs. 435 – 10.15 lakh. A 2 BHK flat of size 707-1533 sq.ft costs Rs. 16.80-39.20 lakh. If you want a bigger house, a 3 BHK flat size 1040-1990 sq. ft can be for around Rs. 26.61-62.09 Lakh. The price depends upon the location, size, specification, amenities of the property.

Other than resale properties that include flats, villas and pent-houses, one can also check out new projects coming up in the area. Most of them are offering either ready-to-move-in properties with the latest possession date being by the end of year 2017.

These are mostly luxury projects offering stylish villas hat range above a crore and offer unique amenities, such as club house, outdoor tennis court, swimming pool, power backup, gymnasium, security and more.

WHY KOMPALLY

The fact that one can get affordable properties in Kompally, has made it a destination of choice for people working in Gachibowli and Hitec City. Buyers profile includes only end-users who want to reside in the property, but also investors from Hyderabad and Secunderabad who eye rental yields on their property.

It is a calm residential area that caters to all kind of basic needs such as vegetable markets, shops, hotel, hospitals and banks, super markets.

KOMPALLY, an upcoming suburb of Hyderabad is about 24 km from Hitec City, 15 km from Secunderabad and 18 km from Punjagutta. The area offers a serene living atmosphere which is fast attracting investors. The area is well connected and has many reputed schools and colleges. The area which used

To be a small village with a good green cover is slowly transforming itself into a center of buzzing activities. The residential sector mainly consists of gated communities. As the area is still developing, a gated community is a good option as it is equipped with all facilities.

Civic infrastructure of the area is well in place and social infrastructure is good. There is no traffic congestion here as this saves a lot of travel time. This is an upcoming area as it's the main highway that connects to Adilabad, Medak, Nizamabad, Kareem Nagar and Ranga Reddy district. Popular landmarks in the area are Runway-9, Satyam Computers, Forest Academy, Apparel Export Park EMRI and Dhola-ri-Dhani.

The closest MMTS station is Bolarm and buses to Medchal, Afzalgunj, Secunderabad and Mehdipatnam ply from the Kompally bus stop. The area has some good schools, hospitals, and market places. The area has gone through a transformation and has become self-sustainable. All daily needs are available in close vicinity. The green cover and quality of people living here make this area very cordial and relaxed. The residents of the area don't mind travelling a bit extra everyday as it well maintained gives them access to great amenities. The garbage disposal van clears the bins on a regular basis and we rarely have water shortage and power cuts. I have noticed that the price of fruits and vegetables here is a bit less than the city's prices. Apart from that the area has every facility one needs.

Affordability is an important factor in residential development. Kompally offers good amenities and is very green, The biggest plus point is that it is very close to my factory in Kalal. The rentals here are really affordable compared to other areas.

This area has housing for high and mid segment buyers and investors. It is also seeing growth in terms of commercial outlets. It has potential and is witnessing a steady growth.

DESTINATION CHANDA NAGAR

Chanda Nagar, with its well-developed social infrastructure, proximity to Hi Tech city and Gachibowli is a good choice both for residing and investing.

PUBLIC VIEW

- Chandanagar enjoys being close to IT hubs such as Madhapur, Kukatpally, Miyapur and Gachibowli and this has attracted IT professionals to stay here.
- Soon Chandanagar will witness online sale of flats. Once started, the Flats can be purchased through online open bidding.
- Chanda Nagar is a prominent location with all basic facilities like hospitals, banks, supermarkets and temples. It is close to Gachibowli and Hitec City, IT corridor. It is connected to the airport and railway station.
- Chandanagar is a great locality to settle in, with schools, hospitals, malls, restaurants in the vicinity. It gives opportunity for a balanced work life. It has got good public transport and commutation facilities.
- Chanda Nagar is a very peaceful locality and well-connected with the other parts of the city. It is connected by trains, buses and public transports. Not just the transport facility but the social infrastructure which consists of schools, banks, ATMs and hospitals is also good.

Chandanagar is located to the north of IT hubs of Madhapur and Hitech city, and is a flourishing suburb in Hyderabad. The area has grown significantly in the last few years and has a balanced mix of residential and commercial market. The area lies on the Mumbai highway and is near Kukatpally, a residential hub to the east and IT hubs Gachibowli and Kondapur to the south. The close proximity to IT hubs has attracted IT employees to this locality. This locality is peaceful, well connected and above all affordable for middle class families. Also, everything one need is within the proximity.

Chanda Nagar has a well-connected road network. The APSRTC buses run from Chanda Nagar to key localities like Jubilee Hills, Secunderabad, Gachibowli and other prominent localities of Hyderabad. The locality is also part of the MMTS train service which connects Chanda Nagar with Begumpet, Kachiguda, Falaknuma, Necklace Road, and many other localities. Share autos are also readily available to nearby places. The Mumbai Highway which passes through Chanda Nagar is a well-developed, 6 lane highway which connects Chanda Nagar with other areas in Hyderabad, and the Outer Ring Road is another important road near the area. The HUDA Colony bus stop, Chanda Nagar bus stop, and Lingampally bus station are some of the important bus stops in the locality. The Shamshabad International Airport is 35 km away from the locality. Hyderabad's main railway station, Deccan Railway Station, is 16 km away from Chanda Nagar, and the nearest station, Lingampally Railway Station, is only 2 km away from Chanda Nagar.

Chanda Nagar also has a well-developed social infrastructure. The area has several hospitals and educational institutions. The Indian School of Business (ISB), International Institute of Information Technology (IIIT), University of Hyderabad are located near Chandanagar while National High School and Bhavans are also located in the area. Chandanagar has good medical facilities with hospitals such as Apollo Clinic, Mythri Hospital, Vasan Eye Carte and many more, Chandanagar also has a bunch of vegetable and fruit markets, grocery shops and supermarkets such as More Vijetha, Heritage Fresh and so on.

Chanda Nagar's residential property mainly consists of apartments. Real estate prices in Chanda Nagar are comparatively FFORDABLE THAN LOCFALITIES LIKE Gachibowli or Madhapur though it has increased gradually over the years. Affordable rentals and proximity to HiTech city and Gachibowli is a major attraction, especially for those employed in IT and ITeS sector.

The construction of the Hyderabad Metro Rail will definitely boost the real estate market of Chanda Nagar. Although Chanda Nagar will not have a metro railway station Miyapur, a neighbourig locality located 5 km from Chanda Nagart, is to be part of line 1 of the Hyderabad Metro. The Metro will give greater connectivity attracting more investors and hence boosting the real estate.

==========

DESTINATION EAST MAREDPALLY

HOUSE HUNTING IN EAST AND WEST MARREDPALLY

Marredpally remains a big favourite of city folk who would prefer living in Secunderabad.

What are the factors that one needs to consider while buying a home? A house that comes under your budget, unit size that suits your requirements adequate water and electricity supply, connectivity convenience, and closeness to social and physical facilities. Hyderabad's Marredpally covers all requirements and offers much more to the buyers.

MARREDPALLY IS INVESTMENT WORTHY

The locality is situated at distance of 2 km from Secunderabad and is known as a residential suburb in the city of Secunderabad. The locality is further divided into East Marredpally and West Marredpally. The main USP of the locality is its connectivity, affordability and the varied options it offers to buyers in both its West and East areas.

EAST MARREDPALLY

Connectivity: East Marredpally is well connected with other parts of the city and within the city via East Marredpally road, Maredpallt Tukaram gate main road. The area is close to Secunderabad Cantonment Board at 2 km and NH 44 at 3 km distance.

Infrastructure: In terms of infrastructure, the area offers good education facilities via affiliated schools and colleges such as Government Institute of Electronics, Sri Chaitanya School, Government Institute of Printing Technology, Auxilium Primary Schools, etc. The social fabric also includes hospitals, grocery stores, petrol pumps and other day to day convenience stores.

Prices: The area offers various housing options such as apartments, plots, builder floors, land and residential house.

Consumer view: Buyers have rated the area 4.5 out of 5 on the basis of offering great environment to live, commuting facilities and infrastructure.

WEST MARREDPALLY

CONNECTIVITY: West Marredpally enjoys good connectivity though road ways and railways. The Hyderabad airport and nearest station is located between 2 to 5 km radius.

Infrastructure: The area is developed with the presence of parks, schools, hospitals, function halls, super-markets and banks. Moreover, the presence of commercial markets such as Begumpet and the suburb, Thirumalgherry is also contributing to the rising demand.

Prices: The area offers varied housing types such as apartments, residential houses, studio apartments, plots, residential houses.

Consumer View: West Marredpally has been rated as 4.8 out of 5 which means the environment, facilities, commuting facilities and physical infrastructure facilities.

With all modern amenities in place along with a quiet charm and a friendly neighborhood that has tales of old and new Secunderabad to be told, East Maredpally has been the residence of choice for many for ages and continues to be so.

A part of Maredpally, East Maredpally is an old sub-urban residential area in Secunderabad. Dotted with parks and known for its calm and quiet atmosphere, East Maredpally can be your choice if family friendly residential solution is what you are looking for. A small area in itself, East Maredpally is surrounded by localities like East Nehru Nagar, Seshachala Colony, addda Gutta, Trimoorthy Colony and Tarakarama Nagar. Some of the important landmarks in the area are Shenoy Hospital, Hanuman Mandir and Nehru Nagar Post Office.

The local gentry mostly consist of businessmen and service holders who have been the residents of the area from as early as 1956 when the neighborhood started flourishing. The best part of living in East Maredpally is its proximity to all modern amenities, yet the locality itself is shielded from the chaos of the city. Most of the residents in the area had been in the area for very long time There are a lot of old independent houses that are still there; however, from early to mid-nineties the area witnessed more and more apartments coming up.

In terms of property, residential houses, stand-alone apartments and residential plots are the available options.

The Sardar Patel flyover connects East Maredpally to West Maredpally. The area enjoys a strategic advantage of being close the Secunderabad railway station which stands at a distance of merely 2 kilometers and the RGI airport is around 33 kilometers away There is also a local bus stand connecting East Maredpally to the rest of the city. The area is in the vicinity of some of the most prestigious schools in the city such as, St. Ann's High School, St. John''s Church High School and Mary's High School. Indira Gaandhi College, Kasturba Gandhi College is also nearby. Apart from educational institutions the area has a number of private hospitals around as well. Other amenities like super markets, movie theatres or eateries are also available in abundance. Earlier there were big kirana stores taking care of the daily needs of the residents. But with departmental stores and super markets trend, those kirana shops have turned themselves into departmental stories.

East Maredpally, on account of being an old residential area has a strong sense of community among its inhabitants. The involvement of the residents in maintaining the civic amenities of the area is significant. It is one of the very few areas left in the city that has a significant green cover and it is the people of the locality who deserve the credit. The GHMC parks in the area are duly maintained by the residents itself which gives the area the lush greenery it enjoys. There is a nursery which also looked after by the locales. Growing up here was like growing up in an extended family. The parks here have so many special childhood memories for residents. Also most families are old residents, it is not that they are cold to new families who come here. It is a very friendly neighborhood for anybody who wants to be a part of it.

KEY TAKEAWAYS

- **East Marredpally is a well-developed area of Hyderabad.d The locality offers varied residential housing types such as flats, plots and residential houses.**
- **The locality has been rated as 4.5 out of 5 in Magic bricks on the basis of offering a great environment, commuting and facilities.**
- **As the area is very near to railway station and bus stations, therefore, many it is preferred by buyers and tenants both.**
- **Construction of the metro is ongoing nearby which at present has created traffic issues. However, in th future, it is expected to be a boon to the real estate.**
- **In terms of social infrastructure, the locality scores high owing to the presence of good hospitals and reputed educational institutions.**
- **Within 3 km distance, the residents can reach the nearest railway station Secunderabad Junction and the nearest bus stop is Jyothi Naga stop. Begumpet Airport is the closest airport.**
- **The locality offers qualitative living conditions with the presence of ample greenery and parks.**

RESIDENTS REVIEW

- East Marredpally is a calm residential locality to live. It is 1.7 km away from Secunderabad Railway Station. 1 km way from multiple hospitals like Apollo, Yashoda and as well known Nursing Homes and Clinics.

- East Marredpally is a busy locality for business and corporate personnel. It is near wholesale and retail market. It is a place to live with family as it has everything that compile a family's needs.

- East Marredpally is a completeldy residential locality, with access to great hospitals, banks, temples and schools in the neighbhourhood. Metro Station expected within 500 meters. Presence of 3super markets, 5 banks, 2 petrol bunks, high schools, colleges at a distance of 100 to 500 meters.

==

DESTINATION LINGAMPALLY

Lingampally with its proximity to the IT hub and good connectivity is making a good option for investors.

OVERVIEW

- Located in the vicinity of IT hub Gachibowli and Lingampally, Serilingampally is a well-developed locality.
- It offers options in gated communities. The major advantage is that it offers lower priced properties as compared to other areas.
- Colonies nearby are Kakatiya Colony, RTC Colony, SBH Colony, Srinagar Colony, Danapur Colony, among others.

RESIDENT'S REVIEW

- Lingampally –Serilingampally is a great place for residing. There are malls, hospitals, schools and parks in the close proximity. Besides, commuting is very easy with airport, trains and buses plying from close by. This location is getting a little denser with more gated communities sprouting up.
- Lingampally is a good residential area that is located at a convenient distance from Hitec City and Gachibowli. Travelling to both these areas is easy and comfortable because of the Lingampally MMTS Station. Quiet, peaceful and clean, it is ideal for people preferring to live close to their workplace.
- Lingampally is well connected by trains, buses and public transports. Other physical and social infrastructure is up to date ensuring the residents are at ease. It is a goof locality to reside.

Lingampally, due to its close proximity to Gachibowli, Hitec City, Nanakramguda, Manikonda, and Kondapur, is witnessing a real estate boom. It has become one of the most sought-after residential destinations as it is proximate to the IT hub. Lingampally is situated in the western quadrant of the city and the rental demand in the area is rising as the locality offers affordable rental accommodations.

Lingampally is a good residential area that is located at a convenient distance from Hitec City and Gachibowli. Travelling to both these areas is easy and comfortable because of the Limgampally MMTS Station. Quiet, peaceful and clean, it is ideal for people preferring to live close to their workplace.

The area has good connectivity due to the Nallagandla flyover which connects to Tellapur area, the MTS frequently plying autos and buses. Lingampally is about 27 km from Secunderabad, 22 km from Punjagutta and 11 km from Hitech City. Better connectivity is one factor which makes Lingampally a good residential choice. The area has good super markets, vegetable market and kirana stores. So household shopping is never an issue here. The closest market area is in Chandanagar which is a few minutes drive.

Lingampally is a peaceful residential area in the western belt of the city and the demand is increasing because of the amenities it offers. The social infrastructure is also good in Lingampally. The area has a num er of schools, restaurants and Hospitals. University of Hyderabad and IIIT are very near to Lingampally.

The area has a majority of independent houses, followed by gated communities and very few apartments and a few gated community projects are underway. Retirees and owners from nearby institutions form a majority of the cosmopolitan population. The colonies nearby are Kakatiya Colony, RTC Colony, SBH Colony, Sirinagar Colony and Danapur Colony.

==========

DESTINATION NALLAGANDLA

Nallagandla with its developing infrastructure and improved connectivity is emerging as a potential residential area offering good rental returns.

The locality will soon get a flyover which is going to address the problem of traffic on the old highway to Mumbai. The flyover is spread over a length of 21 meters with a 7.50-metre carriageway.

The locality is witnessing a lot of repair development in terms of filling of potholes and maintenance of roads. As a choice of residence, Nallagandla seems a good locality for families and has been interesting buyers since last year.

RESIDENT'S REVIEW

People have been staying in this area for the past one year Very clam and serene surroundings and an excellent place to stay. Chanda Nagar and BHEL are nearby shopping places. Commute to Hitec City and Gachibowli is very easy.

Nallagandla is a good location with all basic amenities and ideally located within 2 km from Lingampally station and within 10 km distance from BHEL, University of Hyderabad, Infosys, TCS, WIPO, Microsoft, etc are nearby.

Nallagndla is a relatively new residential option that is fast finding a foothold in the real estate market of Hyderabad. It is sandwiched between Gachibowli and BHEL and has zoomed onto prominence on the real estate radar with the development of IT and ITeS sector. The housing demand provided the stimulus for residential development in the location. The locality is transforming into a full-fledged residential hub due to its developing infrastructure and improved connectivity. Nallagandla's housing demand is mainly from people working in the IT companies and it constitutes nearly 60-70 per cent. BHEL also contributes to about 30 per cent of the housing demand.

Nallagandla is placed between the Outer Ring Road (ORR) and the Old Mumbai Road. As a result, swift connectivity and easy accessibility with all important junctions, Hitech City, Banjara Hills and other parts of the city is a clear advantage. The Rajiv Gandhi International Airport at Shanshabad is 39 km from here and is easily accessible via the ORR.The locality is hardly one km from the Lingampally MMTS station. Nizampet, Miyapur, Beeramguda, Gachibowli and Kukatpally are the neighbouring areas. The locality has all basic amenities such as grocery shops, ATMs, schools and colleges within close distance. The area also houses a number of good schools, colleges, healthcare centers, banks and supermarkets.

The properties available in this locality definitely feature amongst the top five investment destinations as of now as per reports. The average rage is Rs. 4,300per square feet. Interestingly, apartments in Nallagandla hold high rental values. Majority of buyers in the area are IT professionals and the government officials working in BHEL are also raising demand. The rental value of 3 BHK units is between Rs. 20,000-35,000 per month and for 2 BHK units it is between Rs. 12,000-23,000 per month. The housing inventory consists of villas, builder floors, plots and apartments. You can buy a 2BHK apartment in the price bracket of Rs. 26-63.45 lakh with sizes varying from 875-1668 sq.ft. Further, the price range for the 3 BHK apartment is Rs. 40 lakh to over Rs. 93 lakh, sizes varying from 1200-23—sq.ft.

Since the area is undergoing a transformation, the time could be right to make an investment. Currently, developers are opting for this destination as it is comparatively an untapped real estate destination that offers vast land parcels for development. Ever since the new residential development, the social fabric has improved which has also resulted in better roads and infrastructure. As an investor if you are looking to buy a spacious apartment to further reap profitable returns in Hyderabad, Nallagandla can be a good choice.

=========

DESTUBATUIB NAGOLE

Nagole, with its affordability coupled with a green and ample environment is attracting investors. It is emerging as one of the preferred residential destinations after Madhapur and Kondapur.

OVERVIEW

- **Nagole is known as a renowned residential colony in Ranga Reddy, Telangana.**
- **It has been witnessing new developments. The streets are undergoing a makeover as GHMC is using recycled plastic waste mix to lay sroads.**
- **Nagole is known for offering budget homes. Flats, residential houses, plots and villas compose the residential inventory.**

RESIDENT'S REVIEW

- **Nagole is very good locality. The upcoming Nagole Metro Station will boost its rel estate. It is near to RTC bus stop, hospitals and shopping complexes. An ideal place for buyers looking for a relaxed and convenient life.**
- **Nagole is a decent area to live in. Real estate has been booming at an escalated space. Dilsuk-Nagar bus depot is getting shifted here. Rajeev Swagruha's 2000 apartments and Indu Aranya's 300 duplex make Nagole's future real estate market bright.**
- **Nagole is a very calm and peaceful residential locality and near all facilities. It is suitable for a family seeking pleasant evenings. It is near to super markets, schools, hospitals and ATMs. It will soon have a Metro Station.**

Nagole, belonging to the Ranga Reddy district of Telangana is one of the fastest developing suburbs, strategically located between the two commercial hubs of Uppal and MP Nagar. It is located towards the east of Hyderabad. The locality has developed into a prominent residential destination over the years and it is now one of the preferred destinations for settlement. Neighbouring areas include LB Nagar, Ramanthapur, Saroor Naga, Kothapet and Auto Naga. It is a fast growing suburb after Madhapur and Kondapur and is considered the future destination of Hyderabad. The area has ample space and greenery and is free from the hustle bustle of the city.

Nagole is well connected linking various of the city with a number of buses plying in the area. One can reach all major parts of the city within 15 minutes by the 8-lane-wide roads. Nagole is now well known due to the Hyderabad Metro Rail Station and Depot being built up in the area. The area is served by the TSRTC buses. The Rajiv Gandhi International Airport is 27.7 km from the locality via the National Highway 765 and the Inner Ring Road. The Hyderabad Railway Station is at a distance of about 15.8 km, along the NH 163.

Vijaya Gardens, Padmavathi, Sai Raghavendra Nagar-Banglaguda, Ayodya Naarr, Ajay Nagar, Anand Nagar X roads, Adarsh Nagar,, Gayathripuram, Indraprastha, Samathapuri, New Nagole, Snehapuri, Sri Ganesh Nagar, Alkapuri, Sai Nagar, Jaipuri, Srinivasa Nagar, Krushinagar,, Arunodaya Nagar,, Cooperative bank, Venkataramana, Mamathanagar are the colonies located in and around Nagole. Working professionals prefer Nagole over other areas nearby localities such as LB Nagar and Dilsukhnagar as it has direct metro connectivity to their work place. The road stretched between LB Nagar, GSI Banglaguda, Uppal is prominent for the Ganesha idols,. Also, Nagole famous for being a hub of marble and granite stone business in the twin cities.

Nagole real estate is sought-afer due to its developing social infrastructure. It has a number of good schools and hospitals Educational institutions in the locality are Krishnaveni Talent School, Master Grammer High School, Bhavya Grammar High School, Indu International School ad Nivedita High School. Hospitals in the area include Sri Lakshmi Multispeciality Hospital and Research Centre. Sujatha Hospital, SLMS Hospital, Ayu Plus Hospital, Hyma Childrens Hospital and many more.

Nagole has easy access to various facilities like post office, shopping complexes like Big Bazaar and retail stores like Heritage fresh in the vicinity and has many grocery stores, cyber cafes and fuel filling stations. Several new restaurants are being put up to service ones appetite. Nagole also has various elite function halls on the Banglaguda road. It is a fast-growing suburb after Madhapur and Kondapur.

The locality has many villas and apartment based projects. It is known for offering budget homes. Plots, flats, residential houses and villas compose the residential inventory. The rental in the area is also affordable.

DESTINATION VANASTHALIPURAM

Vanasthalipuram is a residential area with a peaceful atmosphere ensconced in greenery.

OVER VIEW

- **Vanasthalipuram is a residential, and commercial area located in the LB Nagar part of Hyderabad.**
- **Ne can find both budget and premium homes and is a popular choice of residences amongst families.**
- **The locality is preferred for offering high level of commuting facilities, good environment to live and everyday facilities. It is an developed area in terms of social and physical infrastructure**

RESIDENT'S REVIEW

- **Vanasthalipuram is very nice locality. It is a good place with no pollution and reachable to all public transport and also connecting with two National Highways Vijayawada Highway and Sagar Highway. Colonies are surrounded with many good parks.**
- **This locality is very good for middle-class and upper-middle class families to reside. It is a very calm and quite place with no disturbances from traffic. Most of the residents are employees. Plenty of ground water is available, therefore families prefer living here.**
- **Vanasthalipuram is decent locality to reside. It is suitable for young and retired people. It is a peaceful area with green parks, markets, hotels, cinema halls, schools. It has easy transport options to airport and railway stations.**

Travelling 13 kms from the heart of the city towards Vijayawada highway takes you to LB Nagar zone where the bustling commercial and residential hub Vanasthalipuram throbs with vigour and excitement of a youth. It is one of Asia's largest suburbs, which is fast transforming to a commercial nucleus with its urban developments. If you are looking for a calm and peaceful environment to live in, with basic amenities within reach. Vanasthalipuram can be a good option. Added to that, affordability and easy commutation makes the locality favourite for residents. Along with apartments and flats, the area also has independent houses unlike other areas in the city.

This locality is very good for the middle class and upper middle class families to reside. It's calm and quiet place without traffic disturbance or pollution.

Vanasthalipuram area has plenty of ground water and also receives water supply from the Krishna River so it doesn't have any major water issues.

The other major residential localities nearby to Vanasthalipuram are LB Nagar, Malakpet and Dilsukh Nagar. Vanasthalipuram is well connected with all parts of the city by means of public transport. Around 250 TSRTC buses ply from the area. All the private and RTC buses towards Vijayawada route stop here. The Mahatma Gandhi Bus Station is 14 km away. The nearest railway station is the Nampally Railway station which is 17 kms from Vanasthalipuram. Rajiv Gandhi International Airport is 29 kms away. Many autos, shared autos and private taxis too are easily available. So, travelling cannot be a problem in Vanasthalipuram.

The locality has many pre-schools, primary and secondary schools such as Bashyam, Lotuslap, Ravindra Bharathi, Eurokids, Loyola and many more. It has eye, dental, ENT and Ahyurveda hospitals such as Max, Prag India, Sri Sai ENT and Allergy clinic, Vinayaka Medical and general store, Lakshmi Ayurvedic Hospital to name a few. One of the important facilities one should see while deciding your residence is hospitals because we can't say who is going to fall ill and at what time.

Vanasthalipuram in that way, is a good choice with a number of good hospitals nearby.

ICICI, State Bank, Canara, Vijaya and Axis bank ATMs are also very nearby. The area also has a bunch of good food spots, parks and theatres. Vanasthalipuram has a large Rythu Bazar near Sampoorna theatre and many groceries and daily needs stores along with other smll businesses dot the stretch. Vanasthalipuram also has branded stores such as Reliance Digital, Reliance Footprint, Kalaniketan, Max fashion and many more. It has a plethora of supermarkets such as More, Heritage Fresh and Reliance Fresh.

Being a commercial hub, office spaces are also abundantly available with a price range of about 1 crore for 2400 sq. ft.

Like every locality, Vanasthalipuram also has an increasing number of residential structures and not many open plots are available. With the completion of LB Nagar-Vanasthalipuram metro route, the property prices in Vanasthalipuram are likely to increase. There is no room for any fresh developments. Mostly any sale of property here is for a second sale.

DESTINATION ADIBATLA

Adibatla, with better connectivity and proximity to major social and commercial infrastructure is an appreciable investment option and provides good living atmosphere.

OVERVIEW

- Adibatla is situated in the Ranga Reddy district in Telangana
- It is majorly known for the presence of Tata Advance System and upcoming Aerospace and Precision Engineering Special Economic Zone (SEZ).

RESIDENT'S VIEW

- Adibatla is a very nice location and is near important locations of the city. The area is 10 minutes to Outer Ring Road. TCS is 10 to 20 minutes' drive to the airport, 30 minutes to LB Nagar and 40 minutes' drive to Hitech City. It is a part of the Information Technology Investment Region Project.

- Adibatla is a very good locality. It is located near Yelimineedu and Tata Aerospace. The venture is about 120 acres township with G.P. Layout. All basic amenities are available nearby the locality. It is strategically located in the outskirts of the city.

- Adibatla is a very nice location. It is near to engineering and medical colleges and close to Outer Ring Road and near Srisailam Highway just 5 minutes' drive to Narayana Medical College.

Adibatla is an upcoming area located in the Southern region of Hyderabad which has emerged as one of the perfect places for investment opportunities Adibatla is barely 6 kms away from the Outer Ring Road and the development of the ORR has enhanced the connectivity to Bongulur, Raviryal, and Sreenagar, further interacting NH-9, Nagarjuna Sagar Road and State Highway -5 (SH-5), and linking Adibatla to Vanasthalipuram, Hastinapuram and Chandrayangutta. Added to that, the land availability in Adibatla has made the locality race in real estate development. With ORR, the demand for the area has increased and as a result, the area is witnessing commendable improvements in the residential and commercial sector.

Adibatla is 20 km away from Slhanshabad, while Sagar Highway and Srisailam Highway are 10 kms and 17 kms away respectively. The closest bus stop is Bongulur Bus stop, situated 3 km from Adibatla and Falaknuma Railway Station lies 17 km away. Air travel is facilitated by Rajiv Gandhi International Airport, which is situated 22 km from Adibatla. With ORR, travelling has become so much easy. Also, with a number of good schools, hospitals, super markets and other amenities, Adibatla is a good locality for families.

The locality is also home for well-established social infrastructure. Few noteworthy institutions including Engineering and Technology, Spoorthy Engineering College and Sri Indus College of Pharmacy lie in the vicinity. A plethora of hospitals such as Om Sai Hospitals, Kamineni Hospital, Yashoda Cancer Institute and Aware Global Hospital are also present. The commercial market is also on par with the localities residential market. Mega Mart, Big Bazaar, D Mart Shopping Mall, and MPM Mall are scattered round the area. An array of stores and eateries also dot the streets surroundings the region. Tata Consultancy Services (TCS), Samuha Aerospace Park, Tata Sikorsky Aero-structures Limited, Tata Lockheed Martin, Aero-structures Ltd, Husys India Campus, Cognizant too have their offices here. With all high-end technological firms and companies, Adibatla is a preferred location for IT employees because of the proximity and connectivity.

Residential plots are the commonly found property type in this locality. The average price value in Adibatla per sq. ft is Rs. 8,120. In the next four years the land value will double up. The rent culture in Adibatla is picking up some momentum, with properties being priced economically. The rental price for house ranges from Rs. 1,500 per month Rs. 20,000 per month. Infrastructure development on the few vacant plots in the area will also attract buyers to invest in land here, while also stirring the interest of many more developers. A few companies would also be coming up soon at the Adibatla. The completion of projects is likely to make Adibatla stand out in new light opening up scope for investors.

========

DESTINATION HAYAT NAGA

Good connectivity, direct access to the ORR has brought this area into focus.

Hayat Nagar is a well-placed locality in Hyderabad with proximity to the Outer Ring Road and NH-44 within a 5-km radius. This ensures smooth connectivity of the area with the neighbouring localities and other work spaces of the city.

In Hyderabad, Hayat Nagar is one of the developed localities in terms of social infrastructure such as schools, research institutions, banks, hospitals and grocery stores.

People have been living here from the past several years and the connectivity of the locality has enhanced owing to the availability of local bus services. NH-44 and ORR are within 3-km distance.

Majority of the people showing interest in buying homes in this locality are professionals working in the near by IT huts and multinational companies.

Good connectivity, strategic location, wll-developed social infrastructure and affordable housing are the encouraging factors for Hayat Nagar as a residential destination. The locality serves as a suburb of Hyderabad and is one of the emerging residential areas of the city. It is a blend of both residential hoes and plotted development.

The strategic location of the area is the main reason for drawing attention of buyers. Considering Hayat Nagar is served by two major roads – ORR and NH-44, within 3 to 5 km radius, the locality provides good connectivity to other areas. Connectivity solely makes the locality a good investment location for future as well.

The Outer Ring Road (ORR) is an easy and the fastest way for people living in Hayat Nagar to reach the city, situated at a distance of 17 km. Major IT and ITeS hotspots of Hyderabad such as Hitech city. Gachibowli and Adibatla are all located within a 20-km radius and are directly accessible via ORR. A number of professionals working in these areas prefer living in Hayat Nagar as it is directly connected with these IT hubs and also offers affordable properties .along with its strategic location, well-developed infrastructure, makes it a preferred residential location. Hayat Nagar is close to various research and educational institutions such as National Institute of Agricultural Extension

Management, Rural Technology Park, Bhartiya Vidya Bhavan Vidyasharam, Tata Institute of Social Sciences, Government Junior College, Telangana Tribal Welfare IIT Study Centre, among others, all within 5 to 7 km radius. Apart from this, banks, health care centers, grocery stores and temples are also located within the locality.

WHAT IS AVILABLE?

Hayat Nagar offers maximum plots and these are available in sizes of 150-280 sq.yard with prices ranging from Rs. 15 to 45 lakh. The locality also offers 2 and 3 BHK residential houses For a 2 BHK house with an average size of 900-1300 sq. ft the price ranges from Rs. 25-50 lakh and for a 3 BHK house, of 1500-2000 sq. ft is available for Rs. 40-65 lakhs.

Good connectivity along with well-developed social infrastructure are the plus points off Hayat Nagar.

=============

DESTINATION – RAJENDRA NAGAR

Good connectivity, direct access to the ORR has brought this area into focus. Rajendra Nagar is a well-placed locality of the city with proximity to Hitec City and Secunderabad. One can find a host of housing options here from gated communities to villas and high-end apartments.

PEOPLE'S TAKE

- Rajendra Nagar is an established locality with proximity to the Hyderabad Airport. The area receives very less traffic as it is only 4 minutes from ORR.
- Rajendra Nagar is a peaceful locality with some development in the last 10 years but there is still room for more. Most of the residential units available here are in large colonies.
- Rajendra Nagar is a convenient location for residing and is close to work spaces. It also has shops, malls, theaters and beauty parlors in the vicinity.
- Rajendra Nagar is best known for affordable homes and green environment. Another benefit is its easy accessibility to nearby developed localities.
- Rajendra Nagar is known for developed residential plots, gated communities, proximity to Hyderabad airport, access to transportation mediums.

One of the upcoming localities in South Hyderabad, Rajendra Nagar has turned out to be a very promising location in the last few years ever since the PV Narasimha Rao Elevated Airport Expressway became functional. The expressway is an 11.6 km elevated stretch, connecting the Hyderabad International Airport with the Mehdipatnam area. This suburb is a 30-minute drive from major areas such as Banjara Hills, Begumpet, Secunderabad and Charminar, Distance-wise, it is only 19 km from the airport and 15 km from the Hyderabad railway station. Location-wise, it lies along the Outer Ring Road (ORR) and is close to NH-7 that connects the city to Bangaore, Srisailam and Nagarjuna Sagar.

This locality is well-connected with the Financial District in gachibowli and the well-known Hitec City. As per reports, the decision of the state government to build 20 flyovers in Hyderabad and allocation of funds to the same will further ease connectivity from Rajendra Nagar to the rest of the city. With the metro rail expected to start operations this year, the nearest Metro station at Falaknuma will be only 5 minutes. Buses also ply regularly within the area to various parts of the city.

Close to the proposed largest underground aquarium by the Tourism department, the area houses the Nehru Zoological Park and the prestigious Acharya NG Ranga Agricultural University, as well as the Kasturba Nature Cure Hospital. There are several established and upcoming schools, health-care centers and hospitals in the vicinity. The pristine Himayat Sagar reservoir is also close by.

Several prominent state and central government institutions also dot the areas, including the Andhra Pradesh Police Academy (APPA), the National Institute of Rural Development (NIRD), National Mineral Development Corporation (NMDC) and others

Apart from connectivity and proximity to the main city and airport, the area has wide roads and good amenities. This self-contained locality receives a healthy demand for residential properties due to the availability of quality husing in all budget categories.

Prominent real estate companies active in the area including Rathi Constructions, Landmark Group, Mars Developers, The Allied Homes, Star Crescento, Dream India Group, Pratyusha Developers, among others.

Investors have a host of options from gated communities to villas to high-end apartments. Property in Rajendra Nagar has built-up areas ranging from 1040-1842 sq.ft. Projecgs offer villas, apartments and plots, with 2,3 and 4 BHK configurations.

In a nutshell, analysts believe that the growth potential of Rajendra Nagar can be compared to what Vashi (Mumbai) or Yelahanka (Bangaluru) experienced over the last 5 to 7 years. Thus, apartments in Rajendra Nagar would serve to be a valuable investment considering that the infrastructure development roadmap in this part of the city is quite promising.

MANTRI PRAGADA MARKANDEYULU

[B.Com, DipBM, PG.DipCA, DipCP.]

HYDERABAD [T S] INDIA

[+91] 9951038802

Email: mrkndyl@gmail.com

CPSIA information can be obtained
at www.ICGtesting.com
Printed in the USA
LVHW050620301122
734192LV00012B/392

9 789356 754287